ADDICTED TO VEGAN

ADDICTED TO VEGAN

VIBRANT PLANT BASED RECIPES FOR ALL CRAVINGS

HANNA BUSCHMANN & MANEL GARCÍA

mango
PUBLISHING GROUP

CORAL GABLES

For permission requests, please contact the
publisher at:
Mango Publishing Group
2850 S Douglas Road, 2nd Floor
Coral Gables, FL 33134 USA
info@mango.bz

For special orders, quantity sales, course
adoptions and corporate sales, please email
the publisher at sales@mango.bz. For trade
and wholesale sales, please contact Ingram
Publisher Services at customer.service@
ingramcontent.com or +1.800.509.4887.

Addicted to Vegan: Vibrant Plant Based
Recipes for All Cravings

Library of Congress Cataloging-in-Publication
number: 2023943711
ISBN: (hc) 978-1-68481-329-2
(pb) 978-1-68481-330-8 (e) 978-1-68481-331-5
BISAC category code: CKB085000, COOKING /
Specific Ingredients / Vegetables

CONTEN

FOREWORD

Gloria Carrión,
La Gloria Vegana

I am thrilled that Manel and Hanna have asked me to write this foreword, as they are two individuals I deeply admire. Their innate ability to inspire is unparalleled, and they infuse a touch of magic into every creation, making them truly one-of-a-kind.

I still vividly recall the day I stumbled upon their work. It was during the infamous pandemic, and their striking Instagram photos featuring my hamburger bun recipe caught my eye immediately. From then on, our conversations on social media became a daily occurrence. Over time, our bond extended beyond the digital realm to encompass our families—or rather, all three families, as Miquel Cuenca's clan (@elveganomarrano) completes this beautiful union.

The urgency of raising awareness around reducing animal product consumption cannot be overstated, and accounts like *Addicted to Hummus* tirelessly champion this cause. By showcasing mouthwatering, nutritious, 100 percent plant-based dishes with an artistic and personal touch, they create a powerful and positive influence on others, all for the collective good of animal welfare and planetary health. Manel and Hanna are true masters in both creating and communicating this message.

Addicted to Hummus's culinary creations are characterized by their originality, vibrant colors, and consistently exceptional results. In this book, you will be treated to Manel and Hanna's finest recipes, each crafted with care and love, accompanied by drool-worthy photographs.

Without further ado, it's time for you to turn the page and immerse yourself in this magnificent cookbook.

Best of luck, Manel and Hanna!

INTRODUCTION

Hi, there! It's Hanna and Manel, and we couldn't be happier that you're holding this book. Manel, a born-and-bred Barcelonian, spent his entire life in the city until he met Hanna, who had relocated to Barcelona for work. Our paths crossed at the same company, unrelated to the culinary world, and from that point on, life moved rapidly. After viewing several eye-opening documentaries about food and the food industry, we transitioned to veganism overnight. Soon after, we left our jobs to work remotely and journey across Asia and Europe in our van. While others hit the waves to surf, we dove into the world of street food. We became relentless "hunters" of these culinary treasures, exploring traditional markets, attending cooking classes, and sampling flavors we had never encountered. Without a clear vision or concrete plans, we began adapting traditional recipes into 100 percent plant-based versions and sharing our culinary creations on Instagram. And the rest is history!

This book aims to demonstrate the deliciousness, beauty, and simplicity of 100 percent plant-based dishes. It is perfect for those seeking culinary adventures, those who enjoy cooking but need a creative boost, and those with limited time for grocery shopping and meal preparation. In these pages, you'll find exciting, entirely plant-based dishes, including many tofu recipes that are irresistibly fun and delectable!

Our cookbook doesn't adhere to a specific theme; the recipes are timeless, and when seasonal fruits or vegetables are used, we provide easy substitution options. Essentially, this book is a compilation of our all-time favorite recipes—those we've prepared time and time again, those adored by our families and friends, and those we never tire of. Although our global travels have inspired many traditional dishes, we must emphasize that none of the recipes are 100 percent traditional. We modify them to our liking, utilize easily accessible ingredients, and craft unique interpretations.

Instead of conventional sections like "breakfast, lunch, and dinner," our book is organized into categories that reflect our daily lives, with food comprising about 99 percent of that experience. It's essential to us that our meals are well-rounded, containing proteins, carbohydrates, and healthy fats. We travelers also require practical, non-messy snacks to sustain us during long journeys. Living with Nalu (our son) and Mali (our furry companion), we prioritize easy recipes that eliminate unnecessary steps or allow for larger quantities. We have a penchant for breakfasts featuring oats and a weakness for sweets. Our friends often invite themselves over for meals, prompting us to whip up quick, impressive snacks. We love hosting these gatherings and cherish the memories made. Our passion for hummus, snacks, hot dishes, sweets, and homemade pizza is evident throughout our first cookbook, a labor of love we are incredibly proud to have completed. Above all, we hope you enjoy it, try numerous recipes, perhaps even embrace our approach to eating, unleash your creativity in the kitchen, and experiment with ingredient substitutions as if you've been doing it your entire life.

After all, we find it fun and hope you will too!

SPECIAL INGREDIENTS

In this book, you'll find widely accessible ingredients; however, we understand that some of them may be unfamiliar. Here, we highlight the most unique ingredients and explain why we use them. We hope you find this information helpful!

Flaxseed oil: A source of omega-3, this oil imparts a fishy flavor to dishes. Store it in the refrigerator.

Sesame oil: Essential for crafting Asian-inspired dishes, though we use it sparingly.

Nori seaweed: Rich in iodine, this seaweed is perfect for sushi and fish-flavored dishes.

Starch: Ideal for both baking and sauce-making, starch adds a crispy touch to tofu. We typically use cornstarch and tapioca starch.

Aquafaba: Aquafaba refers to the liquid from cooked beans, particularly chickpeas, which can be used as an egg substitute; this emulsifier creates a creamier texture in hummus. The term "aquafaba" has gained popularity in vegan and plant-based cooking communities, and it is commonly understood among those familiar with this ingredient.

Natural sweeteners: Options like maple syrup, agave syrup, and coconut sugar serve as sugar replacements in many recipes.

Chickpea flour: Excellent for adding extra protein or replacing eggs in certain dishes.

Liquid smoke: Essential for vegan meat dishes or those with a smoky flavor. If unavailable, smoked paprika can be substituted.

Kala namak: A grayish salt that imparts an eggy flavor to recipes.

Nutritional yeast: Provides a cheesy flavor and contains various nutrients.

Soy sauce and tamari sauce: Staples in our kitchen, these sauces replace salt and deliver a distinct umami flavor. Tamari sauce is gluten-free.

Flaxseeds and chia seeds: Omega-3 sources, ideal for egg substitution in baking or as thickeners.

Meat substitutes: Numerous companies now produce meat, chicken, egg, or fish alternatives. Some recipes include these substitutes for added texture and flavor, but tofu or textured soy can also be used.

Tahini: Indispensable sesame seed paste for hummus, other dishes, and sauces. It is an important calcium source. Lebanese tahini is recommended for its less bitter and more liquid consistency.

Tomato paste: Enhances flavor in dishes like stews, rice, and pasta, as well as some sauces.

Rice vinegar: Perfect for sushi and Asian-style sauces.

Some recipes in this book are labeled gluten-free, making them suitable for individuals with celiac disease or gluten intolerance. However, we always recommend carefully examining product labels for "gluten-free" certification. It's better to be safe than sorry.

EVERY MORNIN SHOULD LIKE TH

SPELT BAGELS WITH HOMEMADE JAM

Despite having excellent bakeries nearby, the urge to make our own bread or rolls sometimes prevails. We have a particular fondness for bagels; they make an ordinary day feel special. And discovering how to make them was such a joy. Did you know that bagels need to be pre-cooked in boiling water? When we set out to make bagels, we usually prepare them in abundant amounts and freeze them as soon as they cool. When the time comes, we pop them in the toaster, stuff them with our favorite fillings, and enjoy!

Yields	Time	Difficulty	Party favorite
8-10	2 hr	Medium	★

Ingredients

4 cups (500 g) of spelt flour

2 teaspoons (10 g) of fresh yeast

1 tablespoon (15 g) of extra-virgin olive oil

1 tablespoon (15 g) of brown sugar or agave syrup

2 teaspoons (10 g) of salt

1¼ cups (300 ml) of cold water

white and black sesame seeds

Mix all the ingredients in a bowl by hand. There's no need to knead, but make sure everything is well incorporated. Cover the mixture with a cloth and let it rest for 45 minutes or until it doubles in size.

Flour your work surface and divide the dough into 8 equal pieces (about 4 ounces or 110 g each). Roll each piece of dough into a ball, coat them with enough flour, and make a hole in the center of each one with your thumb. Stretch the dough to form a ring shape. Repeat the process with all the pieces.

Cover them with a damp cloth and let them rest for another 30 minutes.

Preheat the oven to 410°F (210°C). Bring water to a boil in a large pot.

In groups of 2 or 3, boil the bagels for 2 minutes on each side.

Remove them from the water, cover them with seeds while still wet, and place them on a baking tray.

Bake them for 25 to 30 minutes.

Allow them to cool completely before eating.

Feel free to use any other types of seeds: pumpkin, sunflower, hemp, chia, etc.

HOMEMADE RASPBERRY AND CHIA JAM

Serves 10

Time 15 min

Difficulty Easy

Ingredients

3 cups (400 g) of raspberries

2 tablespoons of chia seeds

juice of ½ lemon

7 pitted dates or **2 tablespoons** of sweetener

You can prepare the same jam recipe with any fruit you wish.
Easy, right?

Cook the raspberries and dates in a saucepan until they start to boil and disintegrate.

Crush the raspberries and dates with the help of a fork. You can use a hand blender if you don't want any remaining pieces.

Add the lemon juice and let it boil again for another 2 minutes.

Remove from heat, add the chia seeds, and mix well.

Cool for 5 minutes before pouring the preparation into a clean jar.

Store the jam in the refrigerator and consume it within a week.

These are our bagel topping ideas, but feel free to experiment with all types of fillings, both sweet and savory.

- Scrambled tofu, vegan cream cheese, and avocado.

- Grilled marinated tofu, lettuce, tomato, and herb cream cheese.

- Peanut butter and jam.

FIVE AWESOME SMOOTHIES

Smoothies are a fantastic and easy way to enjoy a breakfast packed with vitamins and proteins, even on the go. We enjoy creating smoothies with various ingredients at home, experimenting with combinations and flavors to emulate well-known cakes, drinks, or desserts. Here's a selection of our favorites.

Yields	Time	Difficulty	High in Protein	Gluten-Free
~2 cups (500 ml)	5 min	Easy		

TIRAMISU SMOOTHIE

Ingredients

¾ cup (200 ml) of plant-based milk

½ cup (125 g) of plant-based yogurt

1 banana, frozen

2 teaspoons (10 g) of vanilla protein powder (optional)

1 Medjool date, pitted

1 teaspoon of cocoa powder

1 teaspoon of instant coffee powder (or 1 espresso)

melted chocolate

Decorate the inside of the glass or bottle with the melted chocolate and leave it in the fridge for a few minutes.

Blend the rest of the ingredients until smooth.

Pour the smoothie into the glass and enjoy!

You can add more dates or sweeteners to each smoothie until you achieve the desired sweetness. We like using frozen bananas, berries, and cold beverages to keep the smoothie refreshing. In any case, you can always add extra ice cubes.

PINEAPPLE LASSI

Yields	Time	Difficulty	Gluten-Free

2 cups (500 ml) · 5 min · Easy

Ingredients

- **⅓ cup** (100 ml) of light coconut milk (the kind sold in cartons)

- **½ cup** (125 g) of plant-based yogurt

- **¾ cup** (130 g) of pineapple, chopped

- **1 teaspoon** of ginger, grated

- **1 teaspoon** of ground or fresh turmeric

- juice of ½ lime or lemon

- **2 teaspoons** (10 g) of sweetener

- **1** ice cube (optional)

Blend all the ingredients. That's the only secret.

BEETROOT LATTE SMOOTHIE

Yields	Time	Difficulty	Gluten-Free

2 cups (500 ml) · 5 min · Easy

Ingredients

- **1¾ cups** (450 ml) of plant-based milk

- **¼ cup** (50 g) of beetroot, cooked

- **1 tablespoon** (20 g) of sweetener

- **½ teaspoon** of ground cinnamon

Blend all ingredients and pour the smoothie into a glass to enjoy.

If you like to see the separation between the two colors, pour 1 cup (250 ml) of cold plant-based milk into the glass. Blend the remaining ¾ cup (200 ml) with the other ingredients and heat slightly. Then carefully add the warm preparation so the two colors don't mix.

BLUEBERRY CHEESECAKE SMOOTHIE

Yields	Time	Difficulty	High in Protein	Gluten-Free
1/4 cups (300 ml)	5 min	 Easy		

Ingredients

- **½ cup** (125 ml) plant-based milk
- **½ cup** (125 g) of plant-based yogurt
- **2 teaspoons** (10 g) of vanilla-flavored protein powder (optional for added protein)
- **1½ tablespoons** (20 g) of cashews
- **1** Medjool date, pitted
- **⅓ cup** (50 g) of blueberries

Like with the other smoothies, it's as easy as blending all the ingredients.

You can add 1 tablespoon of vegan cream cheese for a more special flavor.

CHAI LATTE SMOOTHIE

Yields	Time	Difficulty
1/4 cups (300 ml)	5 min	Easy

Ingredients

- **⅔ cup** (150 ml) of plant-based milk
- **1** chai tea bag
- **1** banana, frozen
- **1½ tablespoons** (20 g) of cashews
- **1 tablespoon** of chia seeds
- **1** ice cube
- **1** chocolate and peanut cookie (optional)

Brew the chai tea directly in your chosen plant-based milk and allow it to cool.

Combine all the ingredients in a blender and blend until smooth.

Your smoothie is now ready. If desired, add a crumbled cookie and/or peanuts as toppings.

If you don't have chai tea, you can also use 1 teaspoon of mixed spices (cinnamon, cardamom, clove).

OVERNIGHT OATS, SIX WAYS

"I'm an absolute fan of overnight oats and anything that contains oats. Preparing oats for breakfast has become a part of my nightly routine, and I increasingly love trying new combinations. The fact that a delicious surprise awaits me in the refrigerator is one of the best moments of the morning. We have drawn inspiration from six delicious pies for these overnight oats, hence their names." H.

PB & J

BOUNTY

CHUNKY MONKEY

PB&J OVERNIGHT OATS

Ingredients

Serves

1

Time
15 min

Difficulty

Easy

Gluten-Free

- **¾ cup** (70 g) of certified gluten-free oat flakes
- **1 tablespoon** of chia seeds
- **¾ cup** (200 ml) of plant-based milk
- **1 tablespoon** of peanut butter
- **1 tablespoon** of blueberry jam
- fresh blackberries or blueberries

Mix all the ingredients in a jar and let it chill in the refrigerator overnight.

Serve with peanut butter and fresh fruit.

These oats are delicious with any seasonal fruit and jam.

RED VELVET

BROWNIE

APPLE PIE

In preparing these recipes, you can use soy milk for any of them to give this breakfast an extra source of protein.

You might want to omit the sweetener in some of the recipes if you use a sweet or sugary drink, such as oat or rice milk. The plant-based milk and oats will make it sweet enough!

BOUNTY OVERNIGHT OATS

Ingredients

½ **cup** (50 g) of certified gluten-free oat flakes

¾ **cup** (200 ml) of light coconut milk (not canned)

1 **teaspoon** sweetener

2 **tablespoons** of shredded coconut

1 **tablespoon** of chia seeds

a pinch of salt

1 **tablespoon** (15 g) of dark chocolate for melting

Mix all the ingredients except the chocolate in a jar and stir well.

Let it rest for about 15 minutes. Meanwhile, melt the chocolate in a double boiler.

Pour the chocolate over the oat mixture to completely cover it.

Let the mixture cool overnight in the refrigerator or for a few hours until the chocolate solidifies.

When you're ready to eat the oats, crack the chocolate surface with a spoon and enjoy!

CHUNKY MONKEY OVERNIGHT OATS

Ingredients

½ **cup** (50 g) of certified gluten-free oat flakes

1½ **tablespoons** (20 g) of vanilla protein powder

¾ **cup** (200 ml) of plant-based milk

1 **tablespoon** of chia seeds

1 tablespoon of peanut butter

2 **tablespoons** (20 g) of vegan chocolate chips

½ banana, sliced or mashed

a pinch of salt

1 **tablespoon** (15 g) roasted peanuts (optional)

Mix all the ingredients in a jar and let it chill in the refrigerator overnight or for at least 15 minutes.

RED VELVET OVERNIGHT OATS

Ingredients

- **¾ cup** (70 g) of certified gluten-free oat flakes
- **½ cup** (130 ml) of plant-based milk
- **1 tablespoon** of chia seeds
- **⅓ cup** (70 g) of beetroot, cooked
- **1 teaspoon** of sweetener
- **2 tablespoons** (20 g) of vegan chocolate chips
- **¼ cup** (50 g) of plant-based yogurt

Blend the beetroot with the sweetener and plant-based milk. Mix the oats, chia, and chocolate chips in a jar, then add the blended beetroot preparation. You can create layers, as shown in the photo. Store the mixture in the refrigerator overnight. Serve with a generous spoonful of plant-based yogurt.

BROWNIE OVERNIGHT OATS

Ingredients

- **¾ cup** (70 g) of certified gluten-free oat flakes
- **1 tablespoon** of chia seeds
- **1 tablespoon** of cocoa powder
- **¾ cup** (200 ml) of plant-based milk
- **1 teaspoon** of sweetener
- **1½ tablespoons** (20 g) of dark chocolate, chopped
- **1 tablespoon** (15 g) of walnuts, crushed
- a pinch of salt

Mix all the ingredients in a jar and let it chill in the refrigerator overnight. Serve with pieces of chocolate and walnuts.

APPLE PIE OVERNIGHT OATS

Ingredients

- **¾ cup** (70 g) of certified gluten-free oat flakes
- **1 tablespoon** of chia seeds
- **1 teaspoon** of sweetener
- ½ of a grated apple and a little more for decoration
- **¾ cup** (200 ml) of plant-based milk
- **½ teaspoon** of pumpkin spices (or **¼ teaspoon** cinnamon and **¼ teaspoon** ground ginger)

Mix all the ingredients in a jar and store it in the refrigerator overnight.

Serve with a sprinkle of cinnamon and the reserved apple pieces.

If you use baked apples, the result is even better.

Manel likes adding extra protein to his oats; you can add protein powder to your preparations for a protein-rich start every morning.
For a gluten-free version, make sure the oats are certified gluten-free.

TAHINI GRANOLA AND RASPBERRY SMOOTHIE BOWL

If you haven't already noticed, we adore breakfast—especially Hanna! She could eat breakfast three times a day. Granola is a staple in our pantry. We substitute ingredients as we please and use what we have on hand. The beauty of making granola is knowing precisely what's inside. You can control the quantity of each ingredient and craft your own recipe.

TAHINI GRANOLA

Serves
10

Time
2 hr 30 min

Difficulty
Easy

Gluten-Free

Wet Ingredients

⅓ **cup** (75 ml) of tahini (preferably very liquid)

⅓ **cup** (75 ml) of maple syrup

¼ **teaspoon** of vanilla extract

Dry Ingredients

2 **cups** (200 g) of certified gluten-free rolled oats

2 **tablespoons** of chia seeds

¾ **cup** (80 g) of almonds (or pecans)

½ **teaspoon** of ground cinnamon

3 **tablespoons** of coconut, shredded

1 **teaspoon** of salt flakes

Preheat the oven to 300°F (150°C).

Combine the wet ingredients in one bowl.

In a larger bowl, combine the dry ingredients, excluding the coconut and salt. Incorporate the wet mixture and mix well.

Spread the mixture onto a baking tray and press firmly with a spatula. Bake for 12 minutes.

Remove the tray from the oven, add shredded coconut and salt flakes, mix, and press again to form a uniform layer.

Bake for another 12 to 15 minutes until the granola is golden.

Remove the tray from the oven and let it cool completely, which will take about 2 hours.

Break up the granola and store it in an airtight container for 1 to 2 weeks.

You can use any type of sweetener, such as date syrup or agave syrup. However, maple syrup offers the best flavor and makes the granola crunchier.

Any nut butter can be used instead of tahini. However, it should be very liquid, like tahini. If it's not liquid enough, you might need to add oil to the mixture.

RASPBERRY SMOOTHIE BOWL

Ingredients

- **4 cups** (400 g) of frozen bananas, cut into pieces

- **½ cup** (100 ml) of coconut milk or other plant-based milk

- **1 cup** (120 g) of frozen raspberries, plus a few more for decoration

Serves	Time	Difficulty	Gluten-Free
3	5 min	Easy	

In a powerful blender, process all the ingredients except the raspberries set aside for decoration.

Top off your breakfast with granola and the reserved raspberries.

PROTEIN PANCAKES

With a burst of protein and delectable flavor, these pancakes are the perfect way to start your day. Easy to make and delightful to eat, they can be enjoyed with various toppings to suit your taste buds.

Serves **6-8**   Time **15 min**   Difficulty **Easy**   High in Protein

Ingredients

1 cup (100 g) of oat flour

¼ cup (30 g) of protein powder

1¼ cups (300 ml) of soy milk

1 teaspoon of baking powder

2 tablespoons (30 g) of peanut butter

½ cup (80 g) of vegan chocolate chips

oil (optional)

Toppings

Banana

Blueberries

Peanut butter

Maple syrup

Combine the oats, protein powder, and baking powder in a bowl. Add the soy milk and peanut butter and continue mixing until you achieve a uniform batter. Stir in the chocolate chips.

Preheat a pan over medium heat with a touch of oil. Cook the pancakes for 2 or 3 minutes on each side. Serve these pancakes with your favorite toppings. They can be dressed with bananas, blueberries, peanut butter, or maple syrup, among other options.

If you prefer not to use protein powder, you can replace the amount with an additional 1 ounce (30 g) of oat flour.

The pancakes are typically cooked on the inside when they no longer stick to the pan. Flip them and use the same trick for the other side. These sweet treats are the perfect start to any morning.

BAKED OATMEAL: THREE DELICIOUS WAYS

We often crave hot breakfasts, especially in winter. While overnight oats are the most efficient and quick breakfast, sometimes we want something warm, fresh from the oven, and full of flavor and nutrients. We often prepare a large amount of baked oatmeal and freeze it, then reheat it in the microwave when desired. We love playing with flavors, some healthier than others, with varying amounts of sugar and fruits, depending on the occasion and time of year. Which will you choose?

CARROT CAKE-FLAVORED

Serves	Time	Difficulty
1-2	30 min	Easy

Ingredients

¾ cup (80 g) of fine oats

¾ cup (180 ml) plant-based milk

1 small carrot, grated

½ mashed banana

a handful of walnuts

½ **teaspoon** of cinnamon

½ **teaspoon** of baking powder

a handful of raisins

Toppings

vegan yogurt

walnuts

vegan white chocolate

sweetener

Preheat the oven to 350°F (180°C).

Mix all the ingredients well in a bowl.

Place the mixture in an oven-safe dish and decorate with more walnuts. Bake for 20 minutes.

At the end of the cooking time and before serving, add your favorite toppings and enjoy its flavor. You can use the ones we suggest or those you fancy. We like to use soy milk to give it an extra protein boost.

We like to use soy milk to boost the protein.

These recipes are for one or two servings, as we prepare them directly in an oven-resistant breakfast bowl, but you can also make them in a square brownie pan and use double or triple the suggested amounts.

We use different sweeteners for each flavor to provide a distinct sweetness to each preparation. Use these as inspiration, and feel free to substitute the banana with a sweetener or vice versa.

GOLDEN MILK OATMEAL

Ingredients

¾ cup (80 g) of fine oats

¾ cup (170 ml) of plant-based milk

1 tablespoon of date paste

1 tablespoon of almond butter

½ teaspoon of baking powder

1 tablespoon of ground flax seeds

a pinch of pepper

¼ teaspoon of ground ginger

½ teaspoon of cinnamon

1 teaspoon of turmeric

Toppings

banana slices

shredded coconut

maple syrup

Prepare the oatmeal in the same way as the carrot cake–flavored baked oatmeal recipe.

Serve with your favorite toppings.

CHOCOLATE AND RASPBERRY OATMEAL

Ingredients

¾ cup (80 g) of fine oats

⅔ cup (140 ml) of plant-based milk

2 tablespoons of cocoa powder

½ teaspoon of baking powder

1 large piece of dark chocolate

Toppings

1 tablespoon of raspberry jam or sweetener

a handful of fresh raspberries

The steps for this oatmeal are no secret.

Follow the same steps as the previous recipes, but this time, embed the large piece of dark chocolate into the mixture.

Bake for 20 minutes at 350°F (180°C) and, at the end, incorporate your favorite toppings.

SAVORY TOFU SCRAMBLE

Before switching to a 100 percent plant-based diet, we loved scrambled eggs. We didn't eat them daily, but they were a staple for brunches with friends or breakfast at a café. When we became vegan, this was one of the biggest challenges we had to replace. It took several months to discover that silken tofu has a similar texture to eggs.

Combined with firm tofu for protein and kala namak salt, our tofu scrambles have become a beloved dish in our home. We enjoy it for breakfast but also use the scramble as a filling for pastries, pies, or sandwiches.

Ingredients

¾ **cup** (200 g) of firm tofu

¾ **cup** (200 g) of silken tofu

chopped scallion

a generous handful of chopped mushrooms

olive oil

Seasoning

1 **teaspoon** of mustard

1 **tablespoon** of nutritional yeast

¼ **teaspoon** of turmeric

¼ **teaspoon** of garlic powder

¼ **teaspoon** of paprika

1 **tablespoon** of soy sauce (or tamari for a gluten-free version)

Topping

1 teaspoon of kala namak salt

This recipe can also be prepared with other vegetables. Let your creativity run wild!

Serves **2**   Time **10 min**   Difficulty **Easy**   High in Protein

Sauté the scallion and mushrooms with oil for a few minutes until the mushrooms are cooked.

Add the chopped firm tofu and seasoning ingredients, and sauté for another 2 minutes, until the tofu's water has evaporated.

Next, add the silken tofu and stir well for 2 minutes until it reaches your desired consistency.

You can enjoy it alone, over toast, with avocado, or however you prefer. For a complete experience, sprinkle some kala namak salt at the end, imparting that incredible egg-like flavor.

If you can't find silken tofu, you can add a splash of soy milk instead to make the scramble creamier.

BAGELS ON PAGE 16

SAVORY TOFU SCRAMBLE ON PAGE 37

TEMPEH AND VEGAN OMELET BURRITO

Do you enjoy a savory breakfast but don't have time in the mornings? This is the perfect recipe because you can prepare it the night before; in the morning, just heat it in a pan. You can even take it to the office!

Serves — 1
Time — 15 min
Difficulty — Easy
Gluten-Free

Ingredients

1 tortilla wrap

½ cup (100 g) of tempeh

1 teaspoon of soy sauce

½ avocado

beetroot hummus (page 190)

baby spinach or lettuce

vegan French omelet

yogurt sauce (page 94)

1 tablespoon of tahini

Cut the tempeh into thin strips and sauté with a few drops of oil for a few minutes. Add 1 tsp of soy sauce and sauté for a few more seconds.

Heat the wrap for 10 seconds in the microwave or a pan to make it more pliable. Otherwise, the wrap may break when folding.

Add all the filling ingredients you'd like: hummus, lettuce, tempeh, and the vegan French omelet described below.

Fold the wrap to make the burrito. Heat it in a pan to make it crispy. Serve with yogurt sauce mixed with tahini.

VEGAN FRENCH OMELET

Ingredients

¾ cup (200 g) of firm tofu

¼ cup (30 g) of chickpea flour

2 tablespoons (20 g) of cornstarch or tapioca starch

⅔ cup (150 ml) of soy milk or water

½ tablespoon of kala namak salt

a pinch of turmeric

1 teaspoon of baking powder

1 tablespoon of nutritional yeast

Blend all the ingredients together with an immersion blender until you achieve a texture similar to whisked eggs. Heat 1 tablespoon of olive oil in a pan. Pour in a portion of the mixture and spread it out as much as possible. Wait for 2 or 3 minutes, then fold it like a traditional French omelet, or flip it entirely and cook for another 2 or 3 minutes over medium heat.

Once cooked, let it cool for a few minutes to reach the desired consistency. With these quantities, you will be able to make 4 omelets.

WITH BEAN SALAD

WITH VEGAN SALMON AND CREAM CHEESE

WITH VEGAN TOFU BACON, CHERRY TOMATOES, AND ASPARAGUS

SAVORY WAFFLES, THREE WAYS

Serves   Time   Difficulty   High in Protein   Gluten-Free

4   10 min   Easy

Base Ingredients

1 cup (100 g) of certified
gluten-free oat flour

1 cup (100 g) of
chickpea flour

1¼ cups (300 ml) of water

2 tablespoons of olive oil

2 teaspoons of
baking powder

½ teaspoon of salt

¼ teaspoon of turmeric
(optional, just for color)

Preheat the waffle maker.

Mix all dry ingredients in a bowl.

Add all wet ingredients and mix until you have a smooth, lump-free batter.

For each waffle, pour a ladle of batter into the waffle maker and cook for about 7 minutes.

If you don't have a waffle maker, don't panic. You can make pancakes with the same batter and enjoy this breakfast just as much.

WITH VEGAN SALMON AND CREAM CHEESE

Serves   Marinade   Time   Difficulty   Party favorite

2   1 hr   15 min   Easy

Vegan Salmon

2 cups (200 g) of carrots

2 teaspoons of liquid smoke

½ sheet of nori seaweed

1 teaspoon of apple
cider vinegar

1 tablespoon of soy sauce
(or tamari for a gluten-
free version)

1 teaspoon of flaxseed oil

2 tablespoons of water

Steam the carrots for about 10 minutes or until tender but not too soft.

Mix the liquid smoke, soy sauce, olive oil, apple cider vinegar, and maple syrup in a bowl.

Cut the nori sheet into small pieces and add it to the marinade.

Once the carrots are cooked, add them to the marinade, making sure all the slices are well covered.

Let them marinate for at least 1 hour, preferably overnight; the more they marinate, the more intense the flavor.

Serves	Soak	Time	Difficulty	Gluten-Free
4	8 hr	15 min	Easy	

When preparing waffles with vegan salmon and cream cheese, sprinkle some dill on top and drizzle with olive oil.

Vegan Cream Cheese

1½ cups (200 g) of raw cashews

2 tablespoons of nutritional yeast

1 teaspoon of salt

½ teaspoon of garlic powder

water for texture

juice of ½ lemon

aromatic herbs (optional)

Soak the cashews for 8 hours.

Add all the ingredients to a food processor or blender.

Process until you get a delicate cream. Add more water if necessary.

Cool for a few hours before consuming it.

WITH BEAN SALAD

Serves	Time	Difficulty	Gluten-Free	Party favorite	High in Protein
2	5 min	Easy			

Bean Salad

1½ cups (200 g) of black beans, cooked and drained

½ avocado, diced

1 tomato, diced

½ cup (70 g) of sweet corn

½ small onion, chopped

juice of ½ lime

½ teaspoon of salt

some pepper

vegan cheese (optional)

salt to taste

White Sauce

3 tablespoons of plant-based yogurt

1 tablespoon of tahini

1 tablespoon of sweetener

1 teaspoon of salt

1 teaspoon of garlic powder

Mix all the salad ingredients in a bowl.

Prepare the white sauce. To do this, mix all the ingredients well in a jar and shake it. If you prefer a slightly more liquid sauce, add a little water.

Serve this salad on the waffles and add the white sauce.

WITH VEGAN TOFU BACON, CHERRY TOMATOES, AND ASPARAGUS

Serves	Time	Difficulty	High in Protein
4	1 hr	Easy	

Vegan Tofu Bacon

½ cup (100 g) of firm tofu, cut into thin slices

2 tablespoons (30 ml) of soy sauce (or tamari for a gluten-free version)

¼ teaspoon of liquid smoke or **1 teaspoon** of smoked paprika powder

1 tablespoon of concentrated tomato paste

1 teaspoon of maple syrup

¼ teaspoon of Dijon mustard

1 teaspoon of rice or apple vinegar

Mix all marinade ingredients in a container.

Pat tofu dry and place slices on a tray.

Brush slices with marinade on both sides and let them rest. For best results, marinate for 1 hour.

Fry tofu slices in a pan on both sides until golden and crispy. You can also bake them.

This vegan bacon is excellent in sandwiches.

Waffle Toppings

vegan tofu bacon

cherry tomatoes

olive oil

green asparagus

sprouts

salt

Cut tomatoes in half and sauté in a pan with oil on both sides until soft and golden.

Steam asparagus until tender and sauté in a pan for 3 minutes with a little oil.

Add toppings to the waffles and garnish with flaky salt and sprouts.

HUMMUS AND LENTIL SHAKSHUKA TOAST

Serves | Time | Difficulty | High in Protein

4

30 min

Easy

Toast

1 slice of bread

lentil shakshuka

traditional hummus
(page 114)

fresh cilantro

vegan feta cheese

Shakshuka

1 red bell pepper, chopped

1 onion, chopped

3 cloves of garlic, chopped

2 cups (250 g) of
tomatoes, chopped

1½ cups (200 g) of lentils,
cooked and drained

1 teaspoon of cumin

1½ teaspoons of
paprika powder

½ teaspoon of salt

½ teaspoon of black pepper

1 tablespoon of
tomato paste

⅔ cup (150 ml) of water

First, prepare the shakshuka. Sauté red pepper and onion until tender. Add garlic and spices and sauté for 1 more minute.

Add tomatoes, lentils, tomato paste, and water. Simmer for at least 20 minutes. Shakshuka is ready.

Toast the bread and spread some hummus on top. Add a generous amount of shakshuka.

Crumble fresh vegan feta cheese and sprinkle with chopped cilantro. Enjoy!

If you want to use raw lentils, use red or coral ones, which cook faster. Add them with the garlic and spices and continue cooking as instructed in the recipe.

BREAKFAST SUPER BOWL

There isn't always time for a breakfast like this, but we cherish sitting at the table and savoring a hearty meal. In Asia, it's commonplace to have savory dishes for breakfast, a tradition we've warmly adopted in our home. Care to join us?

Ingredients

¼ **cup** (50 g) of quinoa

½ of a large potato or a few baby potatoes

¼ of an avocado

3½ ounces (100 g) of spinach

5 cherry tomatoes

olive oil

salt

2 **tablespoons** of hummus (see page 114)

½ **cup** (100 g) of baked beans

Optional: Hemp seeds, pumpkin seeds, grated vegan feta cheese

Serves	Time	Difficulty	High in Protein	Gluten-Free
4	30 min	Easy		

Cut the potatoes into large pieces and drizzle them with olive oil and salt.

Bake them at 350°F (at 180°C) for 30 minutes or fry in an air fryer until golden.

Cook the quinoa according to the package instructions.

Sauté the spinach and cherry tomatoes in a pan with some oil until soft. Season to taste.

Along with the baked beans, hummus, and avocado, you can prepare your super bowl with your cooked foods. Add the optional ingredients to enrich it even further.

BAKED BEANS

Serves	Time	Difficulty	High in Protein	Gluten-Free
4	15 min	Easy		

Ingredients

2 **cups** (250 g) of white beans, cooked and drained

4 **tablespoons** of concentrated tomato paste or ketchup

oil for cooking

2 **tablespoons** of sweetener of your choice

¼ **teaspoon** of smoked paprika

a pinch of cinnamon

½ **teaspoon** of salt

1 **teaspoon** of cornstarch

3 **tablespoons** of water

In a pan with oil, sauté the cooked beans, tomato paste, spices, and salt.

Mix a teaspoon of cornstarch with 3 tablespoons of water and, together with the sweetener, add it to the beans.

Allow the water to thicken, and they'll be ready to eat.

BAKED BEANS

RECIPES
THE GO

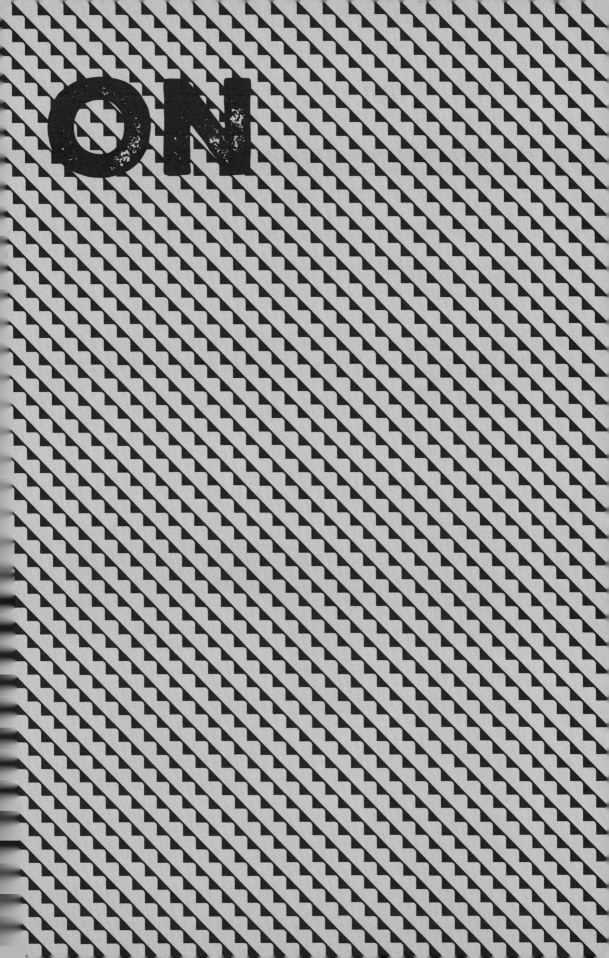

ON

PIZZA MUFFINS

As you might have guessed, we love pizza, but it can be challenging to transport. However, we like to take muffins with us; they're the perfect size for a mid-morning snack and are easy to eat. Muffins don't always have to be sweet; savory ones are just as delicious. Give this recipe a try to see for yourself!

Yields	Time	Difficulty	Party favorite
6	40 min	Easy	★

Ingredients

2 cups (250 g) of wheat flour (you can experiment with other flours if you prefer)

1 tablespoon of baking powder

1 tablespoon of oregano

a handful of fresh basil, chopped

1 cup (100 g) of sun-dried tomatoes (in oil), drained and chopped

a handful of olives cut into small pieces

½ cup (50 g) of vegan cheese, plus a little more for broiling

⅓ cup (75 g) of olive oil

1 cup (250 ml) of plant-based milk (soy milk, for example)

1 tablespoon of concentrated tomato paste

½ teaspoon of garlic powder

salt to taste

Preheat the oven to 350°F (180°C).

Mix the flour, baking powder, and oregano. Add the rest of the ingredients and incorporate them well.

Fill the muffin molds and bake for 25 minutes.

Next, remove the muffins from the oven, sprinkle with cheese on top, and broil.

Let the muffins cool for 10 minutes before removing them from the molds.

You can use the same recipe to make a skillet omelet with the traditional round shape. It's amazing!

SPANISH TORTILLA MUFFINS

Want to surprise everyone at a party or just like having individual portions of potato omelet? This is your recipe! We love that these muffins maintain that egg-like texture on the inside even after baking. They're so delicious it's hard to eat just one. When we made our first potato omelet, which was still far from this recipe, we were so proud that we wanted all our friends to try it, vegan and non-vegan. The response was so positive that we kept developing the recipe to optimize the texture. Now we're sharing it with you!

Yields	Time	Difficulty	Party favorite	Party favorite
6	1 hr 30 min	Easy	★	

Ingredients

4 cups (400 g) of potatoes, cut into small pieces

2½ cups (300 g) of onion, cut into julienne

olive oil for frying

a little salt

2 tablespoons of white wine

Vegan Egg

1¾ cups (400 g) of silken tofu

⅓ cup (40 g) of chickpea flour

2 tablespoons (30 g) of cornstarch

½ cup (100 ml) of soy milk

juice of ½ lemon

¼ teaspoon of turmeric

1 tablespoon of kala namak salt (or common salt)

½ tablespoon of baking powder

In a frying pan with olive oil, sauté the onion for 30 minutes. Add a splash of white wine and salt when it's halfway cooked for a more delicious result.

Fry the potatoes over medium/low heat for about 30 minutes. You can fry them with the onion. Once the potatoes are ready, drain the oil and set them aside.

Mix the vegan "egg" ingredients in a bowl, excluding the baking powder. You can use a hand blender.

Add the potato and onion to the vegan "egg" mixture. Mix well, incorporate the baking powder, continue mixing, and let it rest for 30 minutes.

Preheat the oven to 350°F (180°C).

Grease the muffin molds with frying oil. Fill them and bake for 30 minutes.

Allow to cool completely before unmolding.

Himalayan black salt or kala namak is used because it provides an aroma reminiscent of eggs. It's not an indispensable ingredient, but it will undoubtedly make the omelet more authentic.

VEGAN PULLED PORK SANDWICH

We assure you that when you try this vegan version of the famous pulled pork made with king oyster mushrooms or cardoncello mushrooms, you will love it. The texture is incredibly similar to the original.

Sandwich

bread for the sandwich

10 ounces (300 g) of king oyster mushrooms

2 ounces ounces (60 g) of barbecue sauce

mango mayonnaise

lettuce

pickles

pickled red onion (page 57)

Marinade

2 tablespoons of olive oil

½ tablespoon of garlic powder

½ tablespoon of smoked paprika

½ teaspoon of salt

½ teaspoon of cayenne pepper

Mango Mayonnaise

¾ cup (150 g) of ripe mango

½ cup (100 g) of vegan mayonnaise (page 132)

1 tablespoon of sweetener

Serves	Time	Difficulty
2	30 min	Easy

Start by making the mango mayo. Combine all the ingredients in a jar and process with a hand blender. Set aside in the refrigerator.

Next, prepare the sandwich ingredients. Shred the mushrooms with a fork. Pierce the fork into the stem of the mushroom and pull along; repeat until there is no more mushroom left.

In a bowl, mix the shredded mushrooms with the marinade ingredients.

Sauté the mushrooms in a skillet for about 15 minutes, until they are crispy. Alternatively, you can bake them for 20 minutes at 400°F (200°C).

Pour the barbecue sauce over the mushrooms and sauté for a few more minutes.

Assemble the sandwich with the mushrooms, pickled red onion, pickles, lettuce, and mango mayo.

PICKLED ONION

1 medium red onion

⅓ **cup** (80 ml) of apple cider vinegar

⅔ **cup** (140 ml) of water

1 **teaspoon** (4 g) of salt

2 **teaspoons** (8 g) of sugar

You can prepare the pickled red onion the same day or a few days before. To do this, slice the red onion into rings and press them into a jar.

Heat the water, vinegar, sugar, and salt mixture to dissolve everything. Add the mixture to the jar. Seal the jar and set it aside in the refrigerator to use whenever you like, with a maximum shelf life of 2 weeks.

We love the sweet/salty contrast of the barbecue sauce and mango mayo. Pickled cabbage also works great! When assembling the salad, starting with the dressing and an ingredient that won't get soggy, like chickpeas, pasta, or tofu, is essential. If you start with the leaves, they will get soggy.

THREE TAKE-ALONG SALADS

We love salads so much that we prepare one at least once a day. They are fresh and usually nutritious. We enjoy making salads with whatever we have at home: a good source of protein, fresh vegetables, often fruit, and most importantly, a delicious vinaigrette. Whenever we go on a trip, we like to bring our food. However, take-along salads can be quite a challenge. The best way to prepare our salads is in a jar. Here's a variety of our favorite take-along salads for travel!

PROTEIN BOMB

Serves	Time	Difficulty	High in Protein
1	15 min	Easy	

Ingredients

1 cup (100 g) of lentils, cooked and drained

½ cup (60 g) of quinoa, cooked

3 ounces (80 g) of tofu

olive oil

½ tablespoon of soy sauce (or tamari for a gluten-free version)

½ teaspoon of sweet paprika

¼ cup (50 g) of roasted sweet potato, cubed

½ ounce (15 g) of baby spinach (a generous handful)

a few pomegranate seeds

¼ cup (50 g) of tahini lemon vinaigrette

Tahini Lemon Vinaigrette

1 tablespoon of tahini

1 tablespoon of lemon juice

2 tablespoons of plant-based yogurt

1 teaspoon of sweetener

salt to taste

water to thin the vinaigrette

Dice the tofu and sauté it in a little oil for a few minutes.

Add the soy sauce and sweet paprika. Set aside.

Mix the vinaigrette ingredients.

Assemble the salad with the remaining ingredients and add the vinaigrette.

To enjoy the salad, turn the jar upside down to mix the ingredients. Eat it directly from the jar or serve it on a plate.

ASIAN-STYLE SALAD

Serves	Time	Marinade	Difficulty	High in Protein
1	30 min	1 hr	Easy	

Ingredients

cucumber salad

1 ounce (30 g) of edamame

3 ounces (80 g) of marinated tofu

½ an avocado

1 ounce (30 g) of cooked vermicelli noodles

a handful of baby spinach

Cucumber Salad

1 large cucumber

1 teaspoon of salt

1 teaspoon of sweetener

1 tablespoon of rice vinegar

1 teaspoon of sesame oil

1 tablespoon of olive oil

1 tablespoon of tamari sauce (or soy sauce, if you prefer)

1 teaspoon of grated ginger

Marinated Tofu

¾ cup (200 g) of firm tofu

2 tablespoons of soy sauce

1 tablespoon of toasted sesame oil

1 tablespoon of agave syrup

Toppings

fresh cilantro

sesame seeds

Prepare the cucumber salad. Wash and cut the cucumber lengthwise. Hit it with your hand until it's almost broken. Remove the seeds and cut into small pieces. Put it in a colander and mix with a little salt. Place a heavy object on top and let it drain for about 30 minutes. Mix the rest of the ingredients to make a marinade. Add it to the cucumber, mix well, and let it marinate for at least 1 hour in a bowl. Set aside.

Meanwhile, prepare the marinated tofu. Press the tofu and dry it as much as possible. Cut it into cubes. In a container or bowl, add the tofu and the rest of the ingredients to marinate for 1 hour or a little longer.

Finish by layering the cucumber salad, marinated tofu, and the rest of the ingredients. Garnish with cilantro and some sesame seeds.

MEDITERRANEAN SALAD

Serves
1

Time
30 min

Marinade
1 hr

Difficulty
Easy

High in Protein

Ingredients

¾ **cup** (80 g) of cooked pasta
(for example, fusilli)

1 ounce (20 g) of arugula

½ **cup** (70 g) of
cooked chickpeas

1 ounce (30 g) of sun-dried
tomatoes in oil (about
3 tomatoes)

1 ounce (30 g) of vegan
mozzarella

5 pitted olives

1 **tablespoon** of pine nuts

Vinaigrette

1 **tablespoon** of pesto (page 75)

1 **tablespoon** of extra-virgin olive oil

½ **tablespoon** of balsamic vinegar

Cook the pasta according to the manufacturer's instructions.

Meanwhile, prepare the vinaigrette by mixing all the ingredients.

Place the vinaigrette in a jar and layer in all the salad
ingredients.

MANEL'S SANDWICHES

Manel's sandwiches are a hit in our family. He simply makes the best, most creative, and lovingly prepared sandwiches. He doesn't follow a strict recipe but instead looks in the fridge, takes out some ingredients, and starts making the sandwich; it always turns out amazing. Some staple ingredients are sautéed tofu slices, vegetables, cream cheese, and lettuce. The following recipe is one of Hanna's favorite versions, and we wanted to share it with you:

Serves	Time	Difficulty	High in Protein
1	15 min	Easy	

Ingredients

¼ of a baguette or **2** large slices of bread

4 slices of eggplant, peeled

½ cup (150 g) of tofu, cut into 2 large slices

½ tablespoon of soy sauce

¼ of an avocado, sliced

2 large lettuce leaves

a spread of vegan cream cheese (page 44)

sun-dried tomato paste or pesto

olive oil

Sauté the eggplant slices in a pan with some oil until golden and tender.

Remove the eggplant and let it drain on paper towels.

Add the tofu pieces to the pan and sauté on both sides until golden. Add the soy sauce for a touch of flavor.

Spread the cream cheese on one side of the bread and your favorite pesto on the other slice.

Add the lettuce, avocado, tofu, and eggplant. Enjoy!

VEGAN TUNA SALAD SANDWICH

Serves	Time	Difficulty	High in Protein
4	15 min	Easy	

Ingredients

1 baguette

¼ **cup** (50 g) of pickles, finely chopped

¼ **cup** (50 g) of onion, finely chopped

14 ounces (400 g) of chickpeas, cooked

2 tablespoons of olive oil

1 tablespoon of soy sauce

1 sheet of nori seaweed

½ tablespoon of flaxseed oil

½ tablespoon of sesame oil

2 tablespoons of vegan mayonnaise (page 132)

½ clove of garlic

Heat a sheet of nori seaweed in a dry skillet for 1 minute until crispy and easy to crumble.

In a bowl, mix the chickpeas, garlic, crumbled nori seaweed, and flaxseed oil. Mash the mixture with a fork.

Add the remaining ingredients and mix well. Adjust salt if necessary. Your vegan tuna salad is ready to fill the baguette. Enjoy!

This vegan tuna salad is delicious on its own, in a green salad, or simply with breadsticks.

VEGAN TUNA
SALAD SANDWICH

MANEL'S
SANDWICH

ONIGIRAZU

This is the perfect and unique way to enjoy sushi on the go: a delicious, hearty, and scrumptious sushi sandwich instead of small individual sushi rolls. It's much easier to prepare, wrap, and carry. Plus, it's incredible and will make you the star of the train, office, or picnic!

Ingredients

sushi rice

nori seaweed sheets

avocado

baby spinach

mango

cucumber

vegan cream
   cheese (page 44)

tofu katsu

red onion or pickled cabbage

spicy vegan mayonnaise

Sushi Rice

2 cups (380 g) of short-grain
   rice with **3 cups** (700
   ml) of water

4 tablespoons of rice vinegar

2 tablespoons of sugar

1 teaspoon of salt

Serves	Time	Difficulty	High in Protein	Spicy
6	1 hr	Medium		

Rinse the rice in a colander until the water runs clear.

Place the rice in a pot, add water, and bring to a boil. Once boiling, cover the pot and reduce the heat to low for 15 minutes.

Meanwhile, prepare the rice vinegar mixture, completely dissolving the sugar and salt.

After the rice is cooked, add the vinegar mixture, mix well, and transfer to a tray. Allow the rice to cool completely. Do not cover while cooling.

Before handling the rice, moisten your hands to prevent it from sticking.

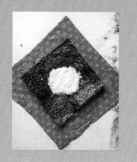

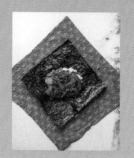

- 1¼ **cup** (300 g) of firm tofu
- 1 **cup** of breadcrumbs
- 1 **cup** of panko (or more breadcrumbs)
- ⅓ **cup** (50 g) of wheat flour
- 2 **teaspoons** (10 g) of cornstarch
- 1 **teaspoon** of salt
- ½ **cup** (100 ml) of water
- ½ **teaspoon** (2 g) of baking powder

TOFU KATSU

To make the crispy tofu katsu, mix all the batter ingredients in a large bowl: flour, cornstarch, salt, water, and baking powder. This batter will create an egg-like texture. Cut the tofu into slices about 0.5 cm (0.2 inches) thick. Prepare a plate with breadcrumbs and another with panko.

Dip each tofu slice first into the batter, then into the breadcrumbs, back into the batter, and finally into the panko. Bake the tofu pieces at 450°F (230°C) for 20 minutes, turning them every 5 minutes.

Oil sprays work great for creating a crispy texture in this type of oven-baked recipe. Alternatively, you can prepare the tofu in an air fryer or deep-fry in oil.

- 2 **tablespoons** of vegan mayonnaise (page 132)
- 1 **tablespoon** of rice vinegar
- ½ **tablespoon** of sesame oil
- ½ **tablespoon** of chili powder
- 1 **teaspoon** of garlic powder
- juice of ½ lime

SPICY VEGAN MAYO

Prepare the spicy vegan mayonnaise by mixing all the ingredients well.

To assemble the onigirazu, follow the sequence of pictures. It's easy! Use the nori seaweed as a base and fold it like an envelope. You can use the ingredients suggested in the first list, combine them, or try other ingredients you prefer.

CRISPY CAESAR SALAD WRAPS

Serves   Time   Difficulty   High in Protein

2   30 min   Easy

Crispy Tofu Fingers

¾ cup (200 g) of firm tofu

1 cup of breadcrumbs

1 cup of panko (or more breadcrumbs)

Vegan Egg

⅓ cup (50 g) of wheat flour

2 teaspoons (10 g) of corn starch (corn flour)

1 teaspoon of salt

½ cup (100 ml) of sparkling water

½ teaspoon of baking powder

Sauce

1 tablespoon of vegan Worcester sauce

1 teaspoon of garlic powder

1 teaspoon of Dijon mustard

1 tablespoon of lemon juice

1 tablespoon of olive oil

3 tablespoons of vegan mayonnaise (page 132)

1 tablespoon of nutritional yeast

2 tablespoons of vegan parmesan

Easy Vegan Parmesan

¾ cup (100 g) of raw cashews

3 tablespoons of nutritional yeast

½ teaspoon of salt

2 tablespoons of extra-virgin olive oil

Finishing

wheat tortillas

lettuce

Prepare the tofu fingers. Press and dry the tofu. Cut it into ½-inch (1 cm) thick strips.

To achieve the vegan egg texture, mix wheat flour, cornstarch, salt, baking powder, and sparkling water in a bowl. Dip each tofu strip into the mixture, then into the breadcrumbs, back into the mixture, and finally into the panko.

Bake at 450°F (230°C) until the fingers are golden, or fry them in oil.

For the sauce, mix all the ingredients until you achieve a homogeneous sauce.

For the vegan parmesan, incorporate all the ingredients in a food processor or blender. Blend until you achieve a texture like grated parmesan.

Assemble your wrap with the wheat tortilla, lettuce, tofu fingers, sauce, and vegan parmesan. You can add tomato if you prefer, or even enjoy the dish as a salad, without the tortillas.

EMPANADAS WITH OUR CHIMICHURRI SAUCE

Serves	Time
8-10	1 hr
Difficulty	Party favorite
Medium	★

This Argentine snack is a favorite of ours; it's the perfect portable food. It reminds us of the afternoons spent reading in Barcelona's Plaza del Sol in the Gracia neighborhood, where we'd always end up ordering empanadas from a nearby place. Once we learned how to make them, we loved them even more. It's a simple recipe, and you can fill them with whatever you like.

Dough

3½ cups (420 g) of wheat flour

4 tablespoons of olive oil

1 cup (240 ml) of lukewarm water

½ tablespoon of salt

4 tablespoons of olive oil

+2 tablespoons of plant-based milk to brush the dough

Filling

1½ cups (270 g) of vegetarian meat, minced

+1 tablespoon of soy sauce

1 onion, chopped

2 cloves of garlic, chopped

¼ cup (50 g) of green olives, pitted and sliced

1 green onion (white and green parts)

½ teaspoon of cumin

½ teaspoon of sweet paprika

1 tablespoon of oregano

½ tablespoon of fresh cilantro, chopped

2 tablespoons of fresh parsley, chopped

Chimichurri Sauce

1 cup (20 g) of fresh parsley, chopped

1 cup (20 g) of fresh cilantro, chopped

1 tablespoon of oregano, dried

2 cloves of garlic, minced

1 tablespoon of ginger, grated

2 tablespoons of red wine vinegar

1 tablespoon of lemon juice

½ cup (120 ml) of extra-virgin olive oil

a pinch of salt

You can start by preparing the filling. To do this, sauté the onion and garlic in a pan until slightly golden. Add all the spices, olives, minced vegetable meat, and soy sauce. Sauté for 5 more minutes. At the end of cooking, add the fresh herbs and set aside.

Prepare the chimichurri sauce. For this, mix the ingredients in a bowl and let it rest for at least 1 hour.

Prepare the dough for the empanadas. Sift the flour into a bowl and mix it with the salt and oil. Pour in the water and knead for 5 minutes until it is smooth and elastic. Add more flour if it's too sticky. Cover it and let it rest for about 20 minutes.

Preheat the oven to 392°F (200°C).

After the resting time, roll out the dough to a thickness of about 1/16 inch (2 mm) on a floured surface. Cut it into 6-inch (15 cm) diameter circles with a mold.

Place a generous spoonful of filling on each circle. Close the empanadas; use your fingers to seal them as shown in the sequence of photographs.

Brush them with the mixture of olive oil and vegetable water, and bake for 30 minutes until golden. Serve them with the chimichurri sauce.

PISTACHIO PESTO ROLLS

These classic rolls are perfect when you're craving a delicious snack to take with you. You can use any pesto sauce you like; the result will be fantastic! You can bake the rolls in a square or round pan, and they will end up sticking together and looking incredible. If you don't have a pan or prefer to bake them as entirely separate rolls, you can also place them on a baking sheet with space between each roll.

Yields	Time	Difficulty	Party favorite
8	2 hr	Medium	

Dough

4 cups (500 g) of bread flour

1¼ cups (300 ml) of plant-based milk

¼ cup (60 ml) of mild olive oil

1 tablespoon (20 g) of sugar

4 teaspoons (20 g) of fresh yeast

1 teaspoon of salt

Filling

4 tablespoons of pistachio pesto

1 cup (100 g) of vegan cheese, grated

You will find the step-by-step instructions on the following page.

In a mixing bowl, dissolve the fresh yeast in the plant-based milk and sugar.

Add the olive oil, bread flour, and salt. Mix and knead for about 10 minutes until you have a smooth and elastic dough.

Shape the dough into a ball and let it rest in the bowl, covered with a damp cloth or a lid, for 1 hour or until it has doubled in size.

Lightly flour your work surface and roll out the dough into a rectangle measuring about 20 x 12 inches (50 x 30 cm).

Spread the pesto over the entire surface of the dough and sprinkle with the grated vegan cheese. See the next page for instructions on how to prepare the pistachio pesto.

Roll up the dough lengthwise and cut it into 8 rolls.

Grease a baking pan and place the rolls next to each other. Cover them with a damp cloth and let them rest for about 30 minutes.

Preheat the oven to 350°F (180°C).

Mix 1 tbsp of oil with 1 tbsp of plant-based milk and brush the rolls. Bake them for 35 minutes.

Let the rolls cool for a few minutes before removing them from the pan.

PISTACHIO PESTO

Ingredients

2 cups of basil (just the leaves)

¼ cup (50 g) of pistachios, peeled

2 tablespoons (30 g) of pumpkin seeds

⅔ cup (150 g) of olive oil

1 teaspoon of salt

1 clove of garlic

2 tablespoons of nutritional yeast

In a food processor or blender, combine half of the olive oil with the other pesto ingredients. Pulse in short bursts to avoid creating a puree. The mixture should maintain some texture. Alternatively, you can prepare the pesto using a mortar and pestle.

Add the remaining olive oil and mix well. Transfer the pesto to a container and refrigerate.

TURKISH
BREAD

TOFU KEBAB ON
TURKISH BREAD

WHITE
SAUCE

TOFU KEBAB ON TURKISH BREAD

This dish reminds us of wild party nights and the subsequent unhealthy food (before we became vegans). In all seriousness, the kebab is pretty decent, especially when made with tofu. Filled with fresh and pickled vegetables, a delicious sauce, and homemade bread, it has become a nostalgic but healthy takeout meal for us!

Serves	Prep	Marinade	Cooking	Difficulty	High in Protein
2	2 hr	1 hr	10 min	Medium	

Kebab Ingredients

about **1 cup** (250 g) of firm tofu

some lettuce leaves

red onion

cucumber or pickles

some tomato slices

white sauce

Turkish bread (page 81)

Marinade Ingredients

2 tablespoons of oil

1 tablespoon of tomato paste

2 tablespoons of soy sauce

1 tablespoon of kebab spice mix

Kebab Spices

½ **teaspoon** of ground cilantro (or coriander powder)

½ **teaspoon** of ground cumin

½ **teaspoon** of smoked paprika

½ **teaspoon** of garlic powder

½ **teaspoon** of black pepper

½ **teaspoon** of ground cinnamon

¼ **teaspoon** of turmeric

¼ **teaspoon** of ground cloves

¼ **teaspoon** of nutmeg

¼ **teaspoon** of ground ginger

1 teaspoon of oregano

Grate the tofu using a coarse grater.

Mix all marinade ingredients in a container or bowl, including the kebab spices. Marinate the tofu in this mixture for 1 hour.

Sauté the tofu in a pan with some oil until it becomes crispy. Alternatively, you can bake it.

Assemble the kebab with ¼ of the Turkish bread (recipe below): lettuce, cucumber, tofu, red onion, tomato, and white sauce.

Feel free to add pickled vegetables or hummus for added flavor!

WHITE SAUCE

Ingredients

3 tablespoons of plant-based yogurt

1 tablespoon of tahini

1 tablespoon of sweetener

1 teaspoon of salt

1 teaspoon of garlic powder

Mix all ingredients in a jar. If you prefer a thinner sauce, add a little water.

TURKISH BREAD

Yields	Prep	Rest
1	5 min	2-4 hr

Baking	Difficulty
15 min	Medium

Ingredients

2 cups (250 g) of bread flour

1 cup (200 ml) of water

1 teaspoon (5 g) of fresh yeast

1 teaspoon (6 g) of salt

1 tablespoon (15 g) of sweetener

2 tablespoons of virgin olive oil

sesame seeds (black and white)

Mix water, yeast, and sweetener in a bowl.

Add flour and salt; mix well. No kneading is required but ensure there are no lumps of flour. The dough will be very sticky; this is normal.

Cover the bowl with plastic wrap, a plate, or a damp cloth, and let the dough ferment until it doubles in volume (2 to 4 hours, depending on room temperature).

Transfer the dough to a well-floured surface and carefully shape it into a ¾-inch-thick round.

Place the dough on a greased baking sheet. Cover it with a damp cloth and let it ferment for another 45 minutes.

Preheat the oven to 480°F (250°C).

With your fingers, form a circle about 1 inch from the edge of the bread, and then make diagonal lines that intersect.

Brush the bread with olive oil and sprinkle with black and white sesame seeds. Press gently so they stick to the dough.

Bake for 10–15 minutes at 450°F (230°C) until the bread is nicely golden.

SAMOSAS WITH YOGURT DIP

Serves	Prep	Rest	Cooking	Difficulty
16	30 min	20 min	30 min	Medium

Filling

2 cups of potatoes (400 g)

½ cup (100 g) of peas, frozen

½ cup (100 g) of crumbled tofu

1 tablespoon of grated ginger

3 teaspoons of Masala spices

1 teaspoon of salt

oil for frying

ground cayenne (optional)

Dough

2½ cups (300 g) of wheat flour

1 teaspoon (5 mg) of salt

4 tablespoons of oil

⅔ cup (150 ml) of water

vegetable water or aquafaba for brushing

Begin by peeling and boiling the potatoes in salted water until they are soft.

Next, defrost the peas and crumble the tofu. In a skillet, add olive oil and sauté the tofu with the ginger and the Masala spices for a few minutes.

In a bowl, combine the mashed potatoes with the peas and the spiced tofu mixture. If the filling appears too dry, add between ¼ to ½ cup (50 to 100 ml) of vegetable beverage.

Mix all the dough ingredients in a bowl and knead for a few minutes until it becomes elastic and not sticky. Form it into a ball and place it back in the bowl.

Cover with a damp cloth and let it rest for at least 20 minutes.

Dust your workspace with flour and roll out the dough until it is about 1/10-inch thick (2–3 mm).

Cut circles of about 4 inches (10 cm) and then slice them in half with a knife. Form a cone with each half.

Add a tablespoon of filling inside the cone and seal it well at the top.

Brush with aquafaba or vegetable water and bake for 30 minutes at 350°F (180°C).

While we prefer cooking the samosas in the oven or air fryer, you can also fry them as traditionally done. This will significantly change their appearance and taste, but they remain delicious.

YOGURT DIP

4 tablespoons of soy yogurt

⅓ **cup** (50 g) of cucumber, diced

a handful of fresh mint leaves

a handful of fresh cilantro

the juice and zest of ½ a lime

¼ **teaspoon** of salt

pepper to taste

Place all the dip ingredients in a hand blender bowl and mix until smooth. This dip is perfect for accompanying these samosas.

If you use Greek soy yogurt, the dip will be thicker; with regular soy yogurt, the sauce is thinner but equally delicious.

VEGAN SQUID-STYLE SANDWICH

Ingredients

2 slices of bread

1 cup (200 g) of
  oyster mushrooms

olive oil

spicy smoked vegan
  mayonnaise

breadcrumbs

Vegan Egg Mix

1 sheet of nori seaweed

1 teaspoon of flaxseed oil

1 tablespoon of soy sauce

½ cup (100 ml) of water

⅓ cup (50 g) of flour

1 tablespoon (15 g) of
  cornstarch (corn flour)

1 teaspoon of baking powder

Spicy Smoked Vegan
Mayonnaise

3 tablespoons of vegan
  mayonnaise (page 132)

1 tablespoon of
  smoked paprika

1 teaspoon of ground
  cayenne (if you
  want it spicy)

1 teaspoon of soy sauce

1 teaspoon of sesame oil

Serves	Time	Difficulty
16	30 min	Easy

Separate the mushrooms into strips by hand. Heat the nori sheet in a skillet without oil until it's dry and crispy. Crumble it.

Prepare the vegan "egg" mixture by mixing all the ingredients well in a bowl.

Fill another bowl with breadcrumbs.

Dip the mushroom strips one by one, first in the "egg" mixture and then in the breadcrumbs.

Brush or spray oil to coat the battered mushrooms.

Bake for 20 minutes at 390°F (200°C) or use an air fryer for 15 minutes at 390°F (200°C) until the mushrooms are golden.

Meanwhile, prepare the spicy smoked vegan mayonnaise by mixing all the ingredients.

Serve the sandwich with the vegan "squid-style" mushrooms and the spicy smoked mayonnaise.

Using the same recipe, you can prepare vegan "fish-style" bites. To do this, skip the breadcrumbs and fry them in oil directly with the vegan "egg" mixture. It's amazing!

To achieve the original flavors, you can fry them in oil, although we prefer this dish baked.

LET'S S
SHALL

CURRY AND APPLE CROQUETTES

These croquettes are so creamy on the inside and crispy on the outside; it's astounding! While croquettes can be somewhat labor-intensive to prepare, they're truly worth the effort.

Serves	Time	Time	Difficulty	High in Protein
20	20 min	12 hr	Medium	

Ingredients

2 cups (500 ml) of soy milk (at room temperature)

½ cup (60 g) of wheat flour

¼ cup (60 g) of olive oil

¾ cup (150 g) of chicken substitute or crumbled tofu

1 onion, chopped

1 clove of garlic, chopped

1 grated apple

1 tablespoon of curry powder

½ teaspoon of turmeric powder

salt and pepper to taste

nutmeg (optional)

Breading

wheat flour

plant-based milk

breadcrumbs (or panko for an extra crispy coating)

Start by sautéing the onion with a pinch of olive oil. Once translucent, add the chicken substitute, garlic, and spices, and sauté for 3–4 minutes. Add the apple and cook for about 10 minutes, until all the water is released.

Prepare the bechamel for the croquettes. Heat 60 g (2 ounces) of oil in a skillet or saucepan. If you prefer, you can use vegetable butter. Add the flour and cook over medium heat, stirring constantly to prevent burning. Add the plant-based milk in 3 or 4 increments. Mix well with a whisk until no lumps remain and keep pouring more milk until it's all incorporated. Once all the milk is integrated, season with salt and pepper. Add nutmeg if you like its flavor.

Pour the bechamel into the previous mixture. Combine well and cook over medium heat for a few minutes until the consistency is creamy.

Transfer the croquette mixture to a container or tray and cover with a lid or plastic wrap to prevent a crust from forming on the surface. Let it cool for 1 hour at room temperature and then refrigerate for about 12 hours.

Next, shape the croquettes. Coat them in flour, then in plant-based milk, and finally in breadcrumbs. If you make more than needed, this is the time to freeze them.

Fry them in hot oil. If you want a healthier version, you can bake them.

The texture improves even more if you freeze them before frying. When baking or frying, do it directly without thawing them.

MUTABBAL

It's easy to confuse mutabbal and baba ghanoush as they are two similar dishes in Arab cuisine. Both share the primary ingredient: roasted eggplants. They differ in dressings and some of their ingredients. The first is a cream, and the second resembles an eggplant salad.

Serves	Time	Difficulty	Gluten-Free	Party favorite
4	1 hr	Easy		

Ingredients

2 large eggplants

3 tablespoons of Lebanese tahini

4 tablespoons of plant-based yogurt

juice of ½ a lemon

salt and pepper

¼ **teaspoon** of cumin

¼ **teaspoon** of garlic powder

Toppings

extra-virgin olive oil

flake salt

sesame seeds

pomegranate

Cut the eggplants in half and make a few cuts. Add some oil and salt. Bake at 390°F (200°C) for 45 minutes or until soft. Remove them from the oven and let them cool completely.

Scoop out the eggplant flesh with a spoon and mash it with a fork.

Add the rest of the ingredients and mix them with the eggplant flesh.

Add the toppings and enjoy it with pita bread (page 110).

If you have a gas stove, an authentic and flavorful way to prepare the dish is to roast the eggplants directly on the flame. The smoky aroma and taste are spectacular.

We usually leave the eggplants in the oven after turning it off. This way, they finish roasting and become soft.

POTATO WAFFLES

Serves

4

Time

20 min

Difficulty

Easy

Gluten-Free

Waffle

4 cups (600 g) of
potatoes, peeled

3 tablespoons of
nutritional yeast

4 green onions, chopped

1 teaspoon of salt

½ teaspoon of garlic powder

Yogurt Sauce

½ cup (100 g) of soy yogurt

¼ teaspoon of garlic powder

¼ teaspoon of onion powder

¼ teaspoon of salt

1 tablespoon of
chives, chopped

juice of ½ lemon

1 teaspoon of sweetener

Start by preparing the yogurt sauce. Mix all the ingredients.

Continue with the waffles. Grate the potatoes. Then, dry them well and press them with a cloth to remove all the water.

In a bowl, add all the other ingredients and mix well.

Heat the waffle iron to medium/high heat and brush it with olive oil to prevent the batter from sticking.

Divide the batter into four, form a ball, and place it in the waffle iron. You can spread it a little.

Close the appliance and press. Cook each waffle for about 8 minutes or until well browned.

Serve the waffles with the yogurt sauce.

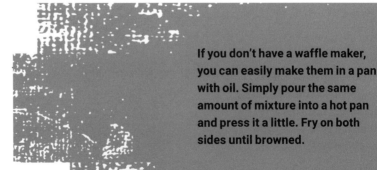

If you don't have a waffle maker, you can easily make them in a pan with oil. Simply pour the same amount of mixture into a hot pan and press it a little. Fry on both sides until browned.

TOFU SATAY

When we traveled to Thailand, we regretted not trying this dish, lovingly prepared on the streets, as we couldn't find a vegan option. That's why we created our own version. Enjoy!

Serves	Time	Difficulty	Gluten-Free	High in Protein	Spicy
4	30 min	Easy			

Ingredients

1½ cups (300 g) of firm, dry tofu

boiled white rice (optional)

lime (optional)

Marinade

3 tablespoons of soy sauce (or tamari for a gluten-free version)

2 tablespoons of concentrated tomato paste

2 cloves of garlic, chopped

a pinch of pepper

a pinch of cumin

1 teaspoon of sesame oil

1 teaspoon of chili or cayenne (optional)

Sauce

1 cup (200 ml) of water

5 tablespoons of peanut butter

a handful of peanuts, chopped

juice of **1** lemon or lime

1 small onion, chopped

1 clove of garlic, chopped

1–2 teaspoons of sweetener

3 tablespoons of soy sauce

1 teaspoon of sriracha

Prepare the marinade by mixing all the ingredients.

Break the tofu into pieces with your hands and marinate it for at least 30 minutes.

For the sauce, sauté the onion and garlic for about 5 minutes. Add the rest of the ingredients and reduce to achieve the desired texture.

Thread the tofu pieces onto skewers (soak them in water for 30 minutes before threading the tofu to prevent burning).

Grill or barbecue the tofu skewers until golden brown.

Serve with the sauce and accompany the skewers with white rice and lime.

If you want a more authentic tofu texture, you can freeze, thaw, and then dry it.

SHIITAKE Á FEIRA

This is our plant-based version of the Galician octopus á feira recipe, a dish with octopus, potatoes, sweet paprika, salt, and plenty of olive oil. You'll be surprised by how similar its taste and appearance are.

Serves	Time	Difficulty	Gluten-Free	Spicy
2	30 min	Easy		

Ingredients

6 cups (1½ L) of water

2–3 medium potatoes, peeled

1 cup (200 g) of fresh shiitake mushrooms (large mushrooms are preferable)

1 piece of kombu seaweed (or another type of seaweed)

1 bay leaf

sea salt flakes

extra-virgin olive oil

smoked paprika from Vera

hot paprika

1 teaspoon of salt

Bring water with a teaspoon of salt to a boil in a pot. Add the seaweed, bay leaf, potatoes, and mushrooms.

After about 20 minutes, when the potatoes are cooked, remove them from the water along with the mushrooms.

Slice the potatoes and mushrooms. Arrange the potatoes on a plate, place the mushrooms on top, and sprinkle with smoked paprika and spicy paprika to taste. Drizzle with olive oil and add a few flakes of salt.

Don't be afraid to add all the olive oil and paprika you desire!

TOFU AND MUSHROOM TACOS

Serves	Time	Difficulty	High in Protein	Spicy
4	1 hr	Easy		

Ingredients for 8 Tortillas

1 cup (110 g) of wheat flour

¼ cup (50 ml) of warm water

½ teaspoon of salt

1 tablespoon of olive oil

Filling

1 cup (200 g) of grated firm tofu

½ cup (100 g) of finely cut shiitake

avocado

pickled red onion (page 57)

Valentina sauce

cilantro

Marinade for Filling

½ teaspoon of garlic powder

½ teaspoon of cumin

½ teaspoon of cilantro

1 tablespoon of concentrated tomato paste

1 tablespoon of oregano

1 teaspoon of hot paprika

2 tablespoons of white vinegar

2 tablespoons of soy sauce

½ cup (100 ml) of water

In a bowl, combine all tortilla ingredients and knead for 5 minutes. Allow it to rest for 30 minutes.

Form 8 balls and cover them with a damp cloth.

Using a rolling pin, roll out each ball into a circle about 0.08 inches thick. Cook each tortilla in a nonstick pan without oil until bubbles appear. Flip and cook for another 30 seconds.

The tortillas are now ready to be filled.

Cover them with a cloth and place them in a plastic bag if you want to keep them for another day.

Mix all the marinade ingredients in a container or bowl. Add tofu and shiitake mushrooms; marinate for at least 30 minutes. Then, fry them in a pan until the water evaporates, and tofu and mushrooms are crispy.

Assemble the tacos with the filling ingredients and enjoy.

CUCUMBER MAKIS

If you need an easy, healthy, and fun appetizer or snack, this is your recipe. Kids love it!

Serves	Time	Difficulty	Party favorite
4	30 min	Easy	⭐

Ingredients

1 large cucumber

vegan cream cheese (page 44)

avocado

tofu

acidic soy sauce

optional: sprouts, nori, mango, etc.

Acidic Soy Sauce

⅓ **cup** (100 ml) soy sauce

3 tablespoons (50 ml) of lemon juice

3 tablespoons (50 ml) of lime juice

3 tablespoons (50 ml) of orange juice

1 teaspoon of grated ginger

On a flat surface, lay out 2 or 3 pieces of paper towel or a clean cloth.

Using a vegetable peeler, create long, thin strips along the cucumber until you reach approximately halfway.

On the paper towel, arrange the cucumber strips, overlapping them slightly.

Cut tofu into long sticks and sauté with a little soy sauce.

Slice avocado thinly.

Spread vegan cream cheese on the cucumber strips and fill about ¾ of the roll with avocado slices (or mango, if preferred), tofu, sprouts, and any other desired ingredients.

Carefully roll it up, making sure it doesn't fall apart. Once the roll is formed, cut it into slices about 1-inch thick. You can use toothpicks to keep them together.

To prepare the acid soy sauce, mix all the ingredients.

Dip the makis in the soy sauce and enjoy.

Fill the sushi rolls with the ingredients of your choice. They always turn out amazing!

MY FATHER'S VEGAN SOBRASADA

This spreadable vegan sausage, originally from Mallorca, is enjoyed throughout Spain for its red color and smoky flavor. "My father never does things halfway. When he pursues something, he goes all out. In fact, he created this recipe and only shared it with us when the flavor was absolutely perfect. This vegan sobrasada is so good and tastes so much like the original sausage that even non-vegans often prefer this version." M.

Ingredients

- **1 cup** (150 g) of sun-dried tomatoes (oil-free)

- **½ cup** (75 g) of toasted almonds

- **½ cup** (125 ml) of olive oil

- a handful of parsley

- **1 teaspoon** of salt

- **1 garlic clove**

- **2 tablespoons** of smoked paprika

- **1 tablespoon** of spicy paprika (optional)

Serves	Soak	Prep	Difficulty
8	1 hr	5 min	Easy

Rehydrate the tomatoes in hot water for 1 hour. After soaking, discard the water completely.

Place all ingredients in a blender or food processor and blend until the desired texture is achieved. It doesn't have to be a pâté.

If using oil-packed dried tomatoes, you will need less oil for the recipe, but you will need 9 ounces of tomatoes in oil.

A Mallorcan sandwich prepared with vegan cheese and sobrasada is an incredible experience.

CHICKPEA PAKORAS WITH CHERRY TOMATO CHUTNEY

This may not be an original pakora or chutney recipe, but it's our favorite version. We love Indian food, spices, and their intense flavors.

Pakora

1 cup (150 g) of chickpea flour

4 green onions, chopped

1 cup (100 g) of carrot, grated

2 cups (300 g) of potatoes, peeled and grated

½ cup (100 g) of onions, julienned

⅔ cup (100 g) of corn

juice of ½ lemon

1 teaspoon of salt

1 teaspoon of garam masala spices (or curry)

Chutney

2½ cups (500 g) of cherry tomatoes

1 cup (200 g) of onion, chopped

2 cloves of garlic, chopped

1 inch (2 cm) of fresh ginger, grated

⅓ cup (80 g) of brown sugar

¼ teaspoon of mustard seeds

1 cinnamon stick

½ teaspoon of cumin

Serves	Time	Difficulty	Gluten-Free
8-10	1 hr	Medium	

Mix all vegetables and spices in a bowl.

Add chickpea flour and knead with your hands.

Let the mixture rest for 10 minutes.

Form small balls, flatten them, and place them on a baking sheet. Bake or air-fry for about 25 minutes at 450°F (230°C), until golden.

If frying in a pan, simply take a small amount of the mixture and place it in hot oil.

The traditional pakoras are deep-fried and turn out to be simply incredible. However, you can choose the cooking method that suits you best: baking them, using an air fryer, or deep-frying in oil.

Place all chutney ingredients in a small saucepan and bring to a boil. Make sure to stir constantly, especially at the beginning, to prevent burning.

Simmer for 30 minutes or until desired consistency is achieved.

After cooking, remove the cinnamon stick, pour the chutney into a jar, and store in the refrigerator.

Use the chutney to accompany the pakoras.

CHICKPEA NUGGETS WITH TWO SAUCES

These nuggets are incredibly versatile. Add spices of your choice for various flavors: with herbs, curry, etc., made with chickpeas, you won't lack protein.

Yeild	Time	Difficulty	High in Protein
4	30 min	Easy	

Nuggets

2 cups (400 g) of chickpeas, cooked and drained

⅔ cup (75 g) of oat flour

1 onion, finely chopped

1 teaspoon of Dijon mustard

1 tablespoon of soy sauce

1 tablespoon of olive oil

1 tablespoon of lemon juice

1 teaspoon each of these spices: paprika, salt, garlic powder, onion powder, and a pinch of black pepper

Breading

⅓ cup (50 g) of wheat flour

1 tablespoon (10 g) of cornstarch

1 teaspoon of salt

⅓ cup (100 ml) of water

½ teaspoon of baking powder

breadcrumbs or panko

2 tablespoons of olive oil

BBQ Sauce

3 tablespoons of ketchup

1 teaspoon of liquid smoke or **1 tablespoon** of smoked paprika

1 tablespoon of sweetener

½ teaspoon of cinnamon

½ teaspoon of cumin

½ teaspoon of garlic powder

Three Mustard Sauce

1 tablespoon of old-fashioned mustard

1 tablespoon of yellow mustard

1 tablespoon of Dijon mustard

1 tablespoon of sweetener

Begin by preparing the two sauces. Mix the ingredients for each sauce well and set aside.

Preheat the oven to 350°F (180°C) and prepare a baking tray.

Continue with the nugget preparation. Sauté the onion in oil until translucent.

In a bowl, mix all nugget ingredients, along with the onion, and mash with a potato masher or hand blender. The mixture should have some consistency, so it's better to use a manual masher.

With your hands, form balls or desired shapes and place them on a tray. Chill the nuggets in the refrigerator for 10 minutes.

Prepare a bowl with the breading ingredients, except for the breadcrumbs and oil, which you will mix separately in another container.

Coat each nugget with the breading mixture, then pass them through the breadcrumbs and place them on the lined baking sheet. Bake the nuggets for 35 minutes or until golden.

Once baked, enjoy the nuggets with the prepared sauces.

ROASTED CARROT DIP WITH PITA BREAD

ROASTED CARROT DIP

Ingredients

2 **cups** (300 g) of carrots

½ **teaspoon** of cinnamon

½ **teaspoon** of cumin

½ **teaspoon** of paprika

1 **teaspoon** of salt

½ **teaspoon** of ginger, grated

juice of ½ lemon

juice of ½ orange

1 clove of garlic

a handful of walnuts

a handful of parsley

a handful of cilantro

2 **tablespoons** of concentrated tomato paste

3 **tablespoons** of extra-virgin olive oil

Serves	Time	Difficulty
4	40 min	Easy

Wash the carrots and cut them into 1-inch (2 cm) pieces.

Place them on a baking sheet with a drizzle of oil, a pinch of salt, cumin, and paprika.

Roast for 30 minutes at 390°F (198°C) and let them cool completely.

Place all the ingredients in a blender or food processor and blend until creamy. Add more oil if necessary. Serve with walnuts and cilantro leaves.

PITA BREAD

Serves	Prep	Rest	Cooking	Difficulty
5	10 min	1 hr 40 min	5 min	Easy

Ingredients

2 **cups** (250 g) of wheat flour

1 **teaspoon** (5 g) of dry baker's yeast

⅔ **cup** (160 ml) of warm water

1 **tablespoon** of olive oil

½ **tablespoon** of sweetener

½ **teaspoon** of salt

In a bowl, mix water, yeast, and sweetener. Let the mixture rest for 10 minutes.

In a large bowl, mix the remaining ingredients well and add the water and yeast mixture. Knead for 10 minutes until you get a smooth and elastic dough. Cover and let it rise for 1 hour or until it doubles in size.

Gently deflate the dough. Cut it into 5 pieces. Form 5 balls and let them rest for 30 minutes.

Preheat the oven to 450°F (230°C) and place the baking sheet inside.

Roll out the dough from each ball and form 5.9-inch diameter breads.

Place the breads on the baking sheet and bake for 4–5 minutes.

Remove from the oven and immediately cover with a cloth.

To keep them fresh for more days, store them in a sealed bag.

Enjoy the pita bread with any of the suggested hummus recipes, mutabbal, or your favorite spreadable dips.

SUMMER ROLLS

Summer rolls are a staple in our summer meals. We love how fresh they are; you don't need to cook them. Crisp lettuce and vegetables, sweet fruit, ripe avocado, and green herbs are essential for making them fresh and high-quality. However, the key to this dish lies in the creamy peanut sauce!

Ingredients

rice paper

lettuce

mint leaves

basil leaves

julienned carrots

julienned cucumber

thinly sliced beets

julienned red cabbage

sliced avocado

sliced mango

thinly sliced strawberries

fried tempeh strips

fried tofu strips

cooked and sautéed rice
   noodles with soy sauce

water

These are our favorite ingredients for these rolls. Mix and match as you like!

Time	Difficulty	High in Protein	Party favorite
15 min	Easy		

Prepare all the vegetables, fruits, and other ingredients on a large plate.

Pour hot water into a plate or large bowl. Dip rice paper sheets one by one in the water until completely covered for about 3 seconds; lay them flat on a plate.

Add the filling of your choice, but don't overdo it, as it can be challenging to roll. Cover the ingredients with one side of the rice paper, fold both sides, and continue rolling until the end.

Cut the rolls into 2 or 3 parts, and they're ready to be dipped in the peanut sauce explained below.

PEANUT SAUCE

To prepare this sauce, you will need 3 tablespoons of peanut butter, 1½ tablespoons of soy sauce, 1 tablespoon of rice vinegar, 1 teaspoon of sesame oil, the juice of ½ lemon or lime, ½ teaspoon of garlic powder, ½ teaspoon of ginger powder, 1 teaspoon of syrup or sweetener, and a little water. Mix them well in a bowl. At first, it seems hard, but persist, and you'll end up with a homogeneous and smooth sauce. If it becomes too thick, add water and mix again. You can sprinkle chopped toasted peanuts, sesame seeds, slices of green onion, or crushed chili on top.

MEZZE WITH HUMMUS, VEGAN LABNEH, & FALAFEL

This assortment of appetizer tapas, characteristic of the Middle East with thousands of ways to prepare and countless possible combinations, is perfect for sharing. Serve it with raw vegetables (cucumber, tomato, carrots), boiled or sautéed vegetables (green asparagus, broccoli), olives, pickles, crackers, and pita bread.

Serves	Time	Difficulty
4	10 min	Easy

Gluten-Free	High in Protein

HUMMUS

Ingredients

- **1¼ cups** (250 g) of chickpeas, cooked
- **¼ cup** (50 g) of Lebanese tahini
- juice of **1** lemon
- **½ teaspoon** of salt
- **½ teaspoon** of cumin
- **⅓ cup** (100 g) water or aquafaba

Process all the ingredients in a powerful blender until you achieve the desired texture.

Serve with a drizzle of oil on top and sprinkle with paprika.

VEGAN LABNEH

Serves	Prep	Time	Difficulty	Gluten-Free	High in Protein
4	10 min	12 hr	Easy		

Ingredients

- **2 cups** (400 g) of Greek-style soy yogurt
- **½ teaspoon** of salt

Mix the yogurt with the salt.

Place a colander over a bowl to collect the water released from the yogurt. Pour the yogurt mixture onto a cheesecloth or a nut milk bag and place it on the colander. Put some weight on top and let it rest in the refrigerator for about 12 hours.

Afterward, the labneh will be ready. Serve with oil, garlic, aromatic herbs, and salt flakes.

BROCCOLI AND SPINACH FALAFEL

Serves	Prep	Rest	Difficulty	High in Protein
20	10 min	20 min	Easy	

Ingredients

1½ cups (300 g) raw chickpeas

1 onion

2 cloves of garlic

1 cup of spinach

4 sprigs of broccoli

a handful of parsley

1 teaspoon of cumin

1 teaspoon of salt

1 tablespoon of baking powder

breadcrumbs

Soak the chickpeas for 24 hours.

In a food processor or blender, combine all ingredients except the breadcrumbs. Pulse to chop everything well, but avoid creating a paste.

Transfer the mixture to a bowl and let it rest for 20 minutes. If the mix is too wet, add 1 cup of breadcrumbs.

Take 1 tablespoon of the mixture and form balls. Fry them in oil or bake them at 450°F (230°C) for 20 minutes or until the balls are golden brown.

TIKKA MASALA PIZZA

This might seem like a wildly creative pizza...and indeed, it is! But it's so delicious that we keep making it. This recipe was born out of the leftovers of a tikka masala. The next day we were making pizzas and thought, "Why not give it a try?" We loved it so much that we created this pizza with surprising ingredients and have been repeating it time and time again. Of course, you can also savor this delightful tikka masala on its own or with rice or potatoes, but we adore it in pizza form.

Serves	Cooking	Rest	Difficulty	High in Protein	Spicy
2-3	1 hr	6 hr	Medium		

Pizza Dough
(for 3 Pizzas)

4 cups (500 g) of bread flour

1 teaspoon (5 g) of
fresh yeast

2 teaspoons (12 g) of salt

1¼ cups (300 ml) of water

1 tablespoon of
powdered turmeric

Mix water and yeast in a bowl until dissolved. Add flour, turmeric, and salt. Combine well until the dough can be transferred to a work surface.

Knead for about 10 minutes until the dough is smooth and elastic.

Place the dough in the bowl, cover with a lid or damp cloth, and let it rest for 30 minutes. Then, divide the dough into 3 equal portions and form 3 balls.

Allow the dough balls to ferment on a tray or in a container, separated and well-covered for 5 or 6 hours at room temperature. Alternatively, you can store them in the refrigerator for 24 hours while they ferment. Remove them from the fridge 4 hours before using and let them finish fermenting. They will be ready to shape, top, and bake.

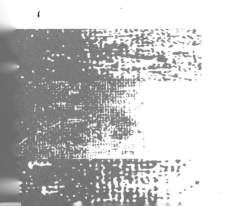

VEGAN TIKKA MASALA

Masala Sauce

½ cup (150 g) of
  tomatoes, crushed

1 tablespoon of concentrated
  tomato paste

⅓ cup (100 g) of coconut milk

½ small onion, finely chopped

1 clove of garlic, chopped

¼ teaspoon of
  ginger, chopped

⅛ teaspoon of cumin

⅛ teaspoon of turmeric

⅛ teaspoon of coriander
  or cilantro

⅛ teaspoon of paprika

⅛ teaspoon of garam masala

⅛ teaspoon of chili

Vegan Chicken or
Marinated Tofu

1 cup (200 g) of vegan
  chicken or tofu

3 tablespoons of plant-
  based yogurt

1 teaspoon of lemon juice

½ clove of garlic, chopped

¼ teaspoon of garam masala

salt to taste

Topping

1 pizza dough

vegan tikka masala

pickled onion (page 57)

plant-based yogurt

fresh cilantro

First, prepare the sauce by sautéing the onion until translucent. Add garlic, ginger, tomato paste, and all spices, and sauté for another minute.

Next, add the crushed tomatoes and continue cooking for a few more minutes. Add the coconut milk and simmer until the sauce thickens. Set aside.

Prepare the marinated tofu by combining all ingredients in a container and mixing well. Add the vegan chicken or tofu, mix, and gently shake the container.

Close the container and let it marinate overnight.

The next day, sauté the vegan chicken or tofu in a pan with oil or bake until golden brown.

Combine the sauce and cooked vegan chicken or tofu.

Preheat the oven to its maximum temperature, in our case, 525°F (275°C) with top and bottom heat.

Roll out the pizza dough and top it with the vegan tikka masala mixture.

Bake for 7 or 8 minutes, until the crust starts to brown.

Garnish with pickled onions, plant-based yogurt, and fresh cilantro.

NO-KNEAD FOCACCIA

Often we think that working with dough and making fluffy bread can be difficult, but this recipe proves otherwise. You won't even get your hands dirty! The key to this recipe is patience and letting the yeast and gluten do their work. You'll get focaccia with incredible flavor and a super fluffy texture. Of course, it's one of our party favorites.

Serves	Prep	Cooking	Difficulty	Party favorite
8	6-9 hr	30 min	Medium	

Ingredients

1⅔ cups (200 g) of wheat flour

½ cup (100 g) of spelt flour

½ teaspoon (2 g) of fresh yeast

1 teaspoon of salt

1 tablespoon of sweetener (agave syrup)

1 tablespoon of extra-virgin olive oil + **2 tablespoons** for greasing the pan

1 cup (235 ml) cold water

Toppings

Sun-dried tomatoes in oil

Kalamata olives

extra-virgin olive oil

Other topping ideas: cherry tomatoes, rosemary, caramelized onions, or flaky salt.

In a bowl, mix the water, yeast, oil, and sweetener. Add the flours and mix well with a spatula or spoon.

Meanwhile, add the salt and continue mixing until the dough is smooth and lump-free. No need to knead; just mix well.

Cover the dough with a damp cloth or a lid and let it rest for 6 to 9 hours at room temperature or until it doubles in volume.

Grease a 9-x-11-inch (22-x-27-cm) rectangular pan with 2 tablespoons of oil. Transfer the dough to the pan and, with your hands greased with oil, stretch it to the edges.

Cover the pan again and let it rest for 1 more hour at room temperature.

After 30 minutes, preheat the oven to 480°F (250°C) with top and bottom heat.

After an hour, drizzle a generous amount of olive oil over the dough and press your fingers into the dough to shape the focaccia.

Top with your chosen toppings and bake for 30 minutes.

Let it cool for a few minutes before removing the focaccia from the pan.

ADDICT
SAVORY

SPICY STICKY TOFU

This recipe and its mango version will make you fall in love with tofu. Promise!

Serves	Time	Difficulty	High in Protein	Spicy
2	20 min	Easy		

Ingredients

1¾ cups (400 g) of firm tofu

4 tablespoons of cornstarch

2 tablespoons of soy sauce

1 tablespoon of sesame oil

Sauce

1 teaspoon of ginger, grated

2 cloves garlic, minced

2 teaspoons of cornstarch

1 tablespoon of soy sauce

2 tablespoons of tomato paste

1 tablespoon of rice vinegar

2 tablespoons of agave syrup

1 teaspoon of sriracha or chili sauce

Toppings

green onion

lime

sesame seeds

Dry tofu as much as possible and cut into cubes.

Mix tofu with its ingredients in a bowl until completely coated.

Heat some oil in a pan and fry tofu until golden on all sides. Set aside.

Mix all ingredients, except garlic and ginger, with ½ cup (120 ml) of water and set aside for the sauce.

Fry garlic and ginger in a pan with oil.

Add the sauce mixture to the pan and cook until it thickens.

Add tofu to the pan and cover it entirely with the sauce.

Serve immediately with rice and add toppings as desired!

STICKY TOFU WITH MANGO SAUCE

Ingredients

1 ripe mango

1 teaspoon of ginger, grated

2 cloves of garlic, minced

juice of ½ a lime

1 tablespoon of soy sauce

1 teaspoon of cornstarch

½ teaspoon of chili (optional)

You can prepare this same recipe with mango sauce. The ingredients are the same for the base and toppings, except for the sauce, for which you'll need the ingredients listed above.

The spicy version is served with white rice, while the mango version is paired with red rice sautéed with soy sauce and bok choi.

SPICY STICKY TOFU

STICKY TOFU
WITH MANGO SAUCE

NO MEAT CHILI LASAGNA

We love giving a little twist to traditional recipes to make them vegan or transform familiar and beloved flavors and combinations into a new, exciting dish! In this case, we used a round pie dish with the same diameter as the tortillas, but you can also use a square dish and cut the tortillas accordingly.

Ingredients

5 wheat or corn tortillas

1 cup (250 g) of crumbled tofu

½ cup (100 g) of red bell pepper, finely chopped

½ cup (100 g) of green bell pepper, finely chopped

1¾ cups (400 g) of black beans

¼ cup (50 g) of sweet corn

1 onion, chopped

3 cloves of garlic, minced

2 tomatoes, chopped

1 tablespoon of tomato paste

1¾ cups (400 g) of tomato puree

2 cups (200 g) of vegan cheese, grated

½ teaspoon of cayenne pepper powder

Serves	Time	Difficulty	High in Protein	Spicy
6	45 min	Easy		

Preheat the oven to 350°F (180°C) and prepare an 8-inch (20 cm) round baking dish. Our tortillas are 20 cm (8 inches) in diameter.

Sauté the onion and garlic in a pan until translucent. Add the peppers and sauté until almost soft. Add the beans, tofu, corn, tomatoes, tomato puree, cayenne, and tomato paste, and simmer for about 20 minutes, until the sauce thickens and the vegetables are soft.

Place the first tortilla at the bottom of the dish and add a large spoonful of the bean mixture on top. Add some vegan cheese and continue with a new layer of tortillas. Repeat the process until the last tortilla and top with the mixture and a generous amount of cheese.

Bake the lasagna until the cheese is golden brown.

Substitute the tofu for ¼ cup (60 g) of texturized soy protein + ¾ cup (150 g) of vegetable broth + 1 tablespoon (15 ml) of soy sauce.

VEGAN MEAT PIE WITH CURRY SAUCE

Pie

2 sheets of round puff pastry

1¾ cups (400 g) of firm tofu

aquafaba or a blend of plant-based milk and oil (for brushing)

Marinade

1 **tablespoon** of soy sauce

1 **tablespoon** of ketchup or tomato paste

2 **tablespoons** of nutritional yeast (or 1 **teaspoon** of dried vegetable broth)

1 **teaspoon** of garlic powder

Filling

1 onion, finely chopped

4 cloves of garlic, minced

2 **cups** (500 g) of mushrooms, finely chopped

1 **cup** (250 ml) of vegetable broth

3 **tablespoons** of cornstarch

½ **cup** (70 g) of breadcrumbs

1 **teaspoon** of salt

½ **teaspoon** of smoked paprika

1 bay leaf

½ **teaspoon** of oregano

ground black pepper to taste

⅓ **cup** (50 g) of toasted peanuts

oil for cooking

Serves	Time	Difficulty	High in Protein
6	1 h	Easy	

Curry

½ **tablespoon** of curry powder

1 **cup** (200 ml) of coconut milk

1 **cup** (200 ml) of vegetable broth

½ onion, finely chopped

2 cloves of garlic

1 **tablespoon** of peanut butter

oil for cooking

Preheat the oven to 350°F (180°C) and prepare a baking sheet.

In a bowl, mix the nutritional yeast, soy sauce, ketchup, and garlic powder. Crumble the tofu and incorporate it well with this marinade.

Spread the tofu on the baking sheet and bake for 30 minutes, until it is dry and slightly golden. Stir halfway through.

Prepare the filling. Sauté the onion and garlic in oil in a pan until fragrant. Add the mushrooms and cook for another 10 minutes. Mix the broth, cornstarch, salt, and spices, and pour over the mushrooms. Turn off the heat, add the tofu, breadcrumbs, and roasted peanuts, and mix well. Remove the bay leaf.

In a 7-inch (18-cm) round pie pan, lay out a puff pastry sheet, letting it overhang the edges. Fill with the prepared mixture and cover with another pastry sheet. Pinch the 2 dough layers together to seal the pie on top, then make small cuts with a sharp knife to let the air escape from the inside.

Brush the top of the dough with plant-based milk and oil or aquafaba for a golden crust. Bake for 30 minutes at 390°F (200°C).

For the sauce, sauté the onion and garlic in oil for a few minutes. Add the curry paste and cook for 1 more minute. Add the remaining ingredients and let it reduce until the desired consistency is achieved.

Drizzle the pie with the sauce and serve warm.

TERIYAKI MEATBALLS

These meatballs will amaze you. They are super easy to prepare and can accompany your favorite sauce. This Asian-inspired version is incredible!

Meatballs

1¾ cups (400 g) of firm tofu

1 cup (100 g) of mushrooms, finely chopped

½ finely chopped onion

2 spring onions (or 1 clove of garlic)

1 tablespoon of soy sauce or tamari

1 tablespoon of a sweetener

a pinch of pepper

1 tablespoon of ketchup

½ teaspoon of salt

1 tablespoon of cornstarch (optional)

chili powder (optional)

rice, spring onions, and sesame seeds (for garnish and decoration)

Teriyaki Sauce

3 tablespoons of soy sauce

2 tablespoons of water

1 tablespoon of maple syrup

1 tablespoon of cornstarch

1 teaspoon of rice vinegar

1 clove of minced garlic

½ teaspoon of grated ginger (from 1 cm piece of ginger)

Serves	Time	Difficulty	High in Protein	Spicy
4	30 min	Easy		

Crumble the tofu. Place it in a cheesecloth or a clean towel and press to remove as much water as possible.

In a bowl, mix the meatball ingredients, except for the cornstarch, which should only be added if the mixture is too wet.

Using a spoon, scoop some of the mixture and form it into a meatball shape.

Once all the meatballs are formed, bake them for 20 minutes at 450°F (230°C), turning them over when they are golden, or fry them in oil.

Meanwhile, thoroughly mix all the sauce ingredients in a glass.

Place the sauce and meatballs in a pan and cook until the sauce thickens and adheres to the meatballs.

Serve with white rice, sesame seeds, and green onions.

You can decide how spicy you want the meatballs: very spicy, slightly spicy, or not spicy. Add the amount of chili that suits you best.

BANG BANG TOFU

Bang! This recipe is dedicated to everyone who still thinks tofu is bland or requires too much work for an acceptable taste. This recipe is one of the easiest, with just a few ingredients. Perfect for spicy food lovers!

Ingredients

1¾ **cups** (400 g) of firm tofu

2 **tablespoons** of cornstarch

2 **tablespoons** of soy sauce

1 **tablespoon** of oil

Sauce

3 **tablespoons** of vegan mayonnaise (or soy Greek yogurt)

1 **tablespoon** of sriracha (or ketchup plus cayenne)

1 **tablespoon** of a sweetener

Serves	Time	Difficulty	High in Protein	Spicy
2	30 min	Easy		

Mix the tofu with the rest of the ingredients. Bake for 20 minutes at 450°F (230°C) or cook in an air fryer for 15 minutes at 400°F (200°C).

Meanwhile, thoroughly mix all the sauce ingredients.

Add the tofu to the sauce and mix well.

You now have an easy recipe ready to enjoy. Serve it with rice, green onions, sesame seeds, and salad leaves.

VEGAN MAYONNAISE

Ingredients

½ **cup** (100 ml) of soy milk

1 **cup** (250 ml) of mild olive oil

a pinch of salt

1 **tablespoon** of lemon juice

½ **teaspoon** of mustard (optional)

Add the soy milk and oil to a blender cup. Place an immersion blender at the bottom of the cup and process at medium speed without moving the head.

When you can hardly see the oil and the mayonnaise has begun to thicken, add the salt, lemon juice, and mustard. Continue processing, slowly moving the head up and down to mix everything well.

For a soy-free option: You can use ⅓ cup (75 ml) of aquafaba, which is the cooking water from legumes, instead of soy milk.

Add half a garlic clove to give the mayonnaise a unique, spicy touch. If you prefer a thinner consistency, use a little less oil.

SILKY TOFU PUDDING

This is a quick way to prepare a super nutritious, fresh, and protein-packed dish.

Ingredients

1¾ cups (400 g) of
silken tofu

2 tablespoons of soy sauce

½ teaspoon of toasted
sesame oil

juice of ½ lime or **1 teaspoon**
of rice vinegar

1 teaspoon of sweetener

1 clove of garlic, minced

1 teaspoon of ginger, grated

Toppings

sesame seeds

cucumber, chopped

green onions, chopped

chili flakes or chili powder

crispy fried onions

Serves	Time	Difficulty	High in Protein
2	5 min	Easy	

First, prepare the sauce. Mix all the ingredients in a bowl, except the silken tofu and toppings.

Place the whole piece of silken tofu on a plate.

Scatter the chopped cucumber and green onions over the silken tofu, according to your preference.

Pour the sauce over the tofu and add the remaining suggested toppings.

WATERMELON VEGAN TUNA POKE BOWL

When you go vegan, you might miss fish, and it's challenging to achieve the taste of fish with 100 percent plant-based ingredients. This recipe will amaze you. Once marinated and baked, watermelon has an incredibly similar texture, appearance, and taste. In a poke bowl, it's a winning combination.

Serves	Time	Time	Time	Difficulty	High in Protein	Spicy
2	6 hr	10 min	2 hr	Easy		

Vegan Watermelon Tuna

4 cups (1 kg) of watermelon, cut into 1-inch cubes

3 tablespoons of tamari or soy sauce

2 tablespoons of mild olive oil

½ tablespoon of sesame oil

1 sheet of nori seaweed

Heat a pan and toast the nori sheet until crispy.

Place the watermelon and all the ingredients in an airtight container or a bag, and let it marinate for 6 hours in the refrigerator.

Next, bake the watermelon without the marinade for 1½ to 2 hours at 350°F (180°C), turning it every 20 or 30 minutes.

While still hot, return the watermelon to the container and let it marinate until ready to serve, preferably overnight.

You can also use this vegan tuna to make sushi. We recommend using at least 2.2 pounds of watermelon, as it will shrink significantly in the oven.

The baking time depends on the size of the watermelon pieces. Keep in mind that it may take longer if the pieces are too thick.

SUSHI RICE

CUCUMBER

MANGO

EDAMAME

TOFU MARINATED WITH SOY SAUCE AND SESAME OIL

AVACADO

CARROT

WATERMELON

SPICY VEGAN MAYONNAISE

Ingredients

2 tablespoons of vegan mayonnaise (page 132)

1 tablespoon of rice vinegar

½ tablespoon of sesame oil

½ tablespoon of sriracha or chili powder

1 teaspoon of garlic powder

juice of ½ lime (or lemon)

There's no secret to preparing this sauce. Simply mix all the ingredients in a glass or bowl and enjoy. If desired, add a little soy sauce or tamari and sweetener for an extra special touch.

For the final touch of this dish, use the following ingredients or substitute them with your favorites: tofu marinated in soy sauce and sesame oil, edamame, mango, cucumber, carrot, avocado, sushi rice, and roasted and marinated watermelon.

SPICY VEGAN MAYO

ASIAN-STYLE NOODLE SALAD

This refreshing Asian salad is one of our favorites because it's packed with flavors, sweet and sour, and reminiscent of the crazy months we spent in Asia.

Ingredients

a handful of lettuce

1 carrot, julienned

½ mango, julienned

a piece of
   cucumber, julienned

½ **cup** (40 g) of mushrooms

½ **cup** (100 g) of tempeh

½ **cup** (100 g) of vermicelli
   noodles (uncooked weight)

a handful of fresh mint

a handful of fresh cilantro

2 tablespoons of soy sauce

Sauce

3 tablespoons of rice vinegar

2 tablespoons of soy sauce

2 tablespoons of lime juice

2 tablespoons of sweetener

2 tablespoons of grated
   lemon grass or lime zest

1 clove of garlic, grated

Serves	Time	Difficulty	High in Protein
1	20 min	Easy	

Toppings

toasted peanuts

green onions

sesame seeds

chili

lime

fried onions

Cook the noodles following the manufacturer's instructions. Once done, rinse them under cold water to stop the cooking process.

Mix the sauce ingredients by pouring them into a jar and shaking it.

Sauté the tempeh and cut into strips with a little soy sauce.

Sauté the mushrooms with 1 tablespoon of soy sauce.

Assemble the salad with vegetables, noodles, tempeh, mushrooms, and herbs. Add the toppings and sauce.

You can use tofu instead of tempeh and substitute the ingredients as desired. That's the beauty of these salads!

CAULIFLOWER TABBOULEH

Is cauliflower a superfood? We don't know for sure, but it's a vegetable packed with vitamins and minerals. Just ½ cup of cauliflower covers half the daily required vitamin C intake for adults! We love eating it steamed, roasted, or even raw!

Ingredients

3 cups (300 g) of cauliflower

1 cup (150 g) of crumbled tofu

¼ cup (30 g) of raisins or chopped dates

seeds from ½ a pomegranate

2 inches (5 cm) of cucumber, chopped

1 carrot, grated

olive oil

a handful of parsley, chopped

a handful of mint, chopped

10 almonds, chopped

½ teaspoon of cumin

1 teaspoon of cinnamon

1 teaspoon of paprika

1 teaspoon of salt

black pepper to taste

Serves	Time	Difficulty	Gluten-Free
2-3	15 min	Easy	

Dressing

juice and zest of ½ an orange

2 tablespoons of oil

½ tablespoon of apple cider vinegar

1 tablespoon of sweetener

Cut the cauliflower into pieces and grate them using a manual grater or food processor until they resemble couscous.

Heat some oil in a skillet and sauté the cauliflower couscous with the crumbled tofu and spices for about 5 minutes.

Let it cool, then mix the cauliflower mixture with the rest of the ingredients in a bowl.

Combine the sauce ingredients in a jar and serve the cauliflower tabbouleh with the dressing on top.

You can enjoy this dish as a raw salad. If so, skip the step where you fry the cauliflower and tofu in the skillet.

TEX-MEX PASTA SALAD

Salad

2¼ cups (250 g) of pasta

½ red bell pepper

½ green bell pepper

½ yellow bell pepper

½ red onion

⅔ cup (100 g) of sweet corn

1½ cups (300 g) of beans, cooked

cilantro

Avocado Sauce

1 avocado

juice of **1** lime

3 tablespoons of soy yogurt

1 tablespoon of fresh cilantro

½ clove of garlic

¼ teaspoon of cumin

1 tablespoon of olive oil

salt to taste

3 tablespoons of water

Toppings

nachos

jalapeños

vegan cheese

chipotle or Valentina sauce (optional)

paprika

Serves.	~Time	Difficulty	High in Protein
4	20 min	Easy	

Cook the pasta following the manufacturer's instructions.

Cut the bell peppers into 0.4-inch pieces. Chop the onion.

Place all salad ingredients in a large bowl and mix.

For the sauce, add all the ingredients to a blender and process.

Serve the salad in four bowls with avocado sauce, nachos, vegan cheese, jalapeños, and paprika.

LEMON AND BAY LEAF RISOTTO

Ingredients

1¼ cups (250 g) of Arborio rice (special for risotto)

juice and zest of **1** lemon

4¼ cups (1 l) of vegetable broth

a little less than **½ cup** (100 ml) of white wine

2 bay leaves

3 cloves of garlic, chopped

1 onion, chopped

2 tablespoons of olive oil

2 tablespoons of nutritional yeast (optional)

Toppings

green asparagus

chives, chopped

Serves	Time	Difficulty	Gluten-Free
2-3	30 min	Easy	

Heat 2 tablespoons of oil in a pot and sauté the onion for a few minutes until translucent. Add the garlic and sauté for another 2 or 3 minutes over medium heat. Pour in 3½ fluid ounces (100 ml) of white wine and let it reduce for a few minutes until all the liquid has evaporated.

Add the Arborio rice (special for risotto) and bay leaves, and stir for a few minutes.

The most crucial step is gradually adding the hot broth to the rice. Cover the rice completely with the broth and keep stirring. When the broth has almost been absorbed, add more broth in the same manner and continue this process for about 15 minutes until the rice is fully cooked, stirring constantly.

Once the rice is cooked, turn off the heat and add the lemon juice, lemon zest, and nutritional yeast. Adjust the salt if necessary (depending on the broth). Stir until well combined.

Cover and rest for 3 minutes while you sauté the asparagus with salt and oil.

Serve the risotto with more lemon zest and chives.

Use vegan butter at the end for an even creamier result.

The amount of broth may be more or less, depending on the process.

ONE-POT CURRY PASTA

This dish couldn't be easier and creamier. We love one-pot recipes, which involve cooking all the ingredients in a single pot. Not only does it save you from cleaning multiple dishes, but you also get a delicious homemade meal!

Ingredients

3 cups (300 g) of pasta

3 cloves of garlic, chopped

1 cup (100 g) of shiitake mushrooms, sliced (or other mushrooms)

2 cups (50 g) of fresh spinach

2 tablespoons of oil

2 ½ cups (600 ml) of vegetable broth

1⅔ cups (400 ml) of coconut milk, canned

1 tablespoon of curry powder

salt

oil

Serves **3-4** Time **15 min** Difficulty **Easy**

Heat oil in a pot and sauté the mushrooms for a few minutes. Add the garlic and curry powder, and sauté for a few more minutes. Then, add the vegetable broth, coconut milk, and spinach and bring to a boil. Season with salt to taste (depending on the saltiness of the broth) and add the pasta. We usually use linguine.

Cook while stirring constantly for 12–15 minutes, until the broth reduces to a super creamy sauce. That's why we recommend using pasta that requires about 10–12 minutes of cooking time.

If you wish to add protein, you can accompany it with crispy tempeh. For this, use ½ cup (100 g) of tempeh, 1 tablespoon of soy sauce, 1 tablespoon of sweetener, and 1 tablespoon of water. Cut the tempeh into small slices. Mix all the sauce ingredients in a jar. Sauté the tempeh in a pan for a few minutes until golden. Pour the sauce over the tempeh and cook for a few more minutes until glazed.

We recommend consuming this dish immediately (perhaps even straight from the pot!). It will never be as creamy as it is right after cooking.

PROTEIN-PACKED ALFREDO PASTA

This is our protein-rich, vegan, and healthy version of the famous Italian pasta with Alfredo sauce.

Ingredients

3 cups (300 g) pasta

a handful of cashews

1½ cups (200 g) of cooked beans

2 tablespoons of nutritional yeast

½ teaspoon of garlic powder

½ teaspoon of salt

⅓ cup (100 ml) of plant-based milk (we use soy milk for an extra protein boost)

⅓ cup (100 ml) of pasta cooking water

Toppings

fresh chives

vegan parmesan (page 69)

Serves	Time	Difficulty	High in Protein
3-4	15 min	Easy	

Cook the pasta according to package instructions and reserve some cooking water.

Process all the ingredients, except for the pasta, including the pasta cooking water, using a hand blender or a countertop blender, until you have a smooth liquid sauce. Add more soy milk if you want a thinner consistency.

Add the sauce to the pot with the pasta and heat everything together. The sauce will thicken slightly.

Serve with fresh chives.

To add more protein to the dish, you can sauté some tempeh or thinly sliced tofu with soy sauce. Another option is to use legume-based pasta, such as lentils, chickpeas, beans, etc. These are high in protein and pair perfectly with this sauce.

PASTA WITH ROMESCO SAUCE AND ARTICHOKES

"In Catalonia, this sauce is very popular and is usually consumed with calçots or grilled vegetables. This is my father's recipe. It always reminds me of when we had calçotadas and gathered the whole family; my grandmother would devour this sauce." M.

Serves 3   Time 35 min   Difficulty Easy

Ingredients

2¼ cups (250 g) pasta

2 artichokes

Romesco sauce

olive oil

salt

Cook the pasta and reserve some cooking water.

Remove the stem and outer leaves from the artichokes. Cut off the top and bottom, leaving only the heart. Slice them into about ⅛-inch (3 mm) thick pieces. Place the artichokes in a bowl, add 1 tablespoon of oil and some salt, and gently mix to avoid breaking them. Bake for 15 minutes at 390°F (200°C) or until crispy. You can also fry them in oil or use an air fryer.

Once the pasta is drained, put it back in the pot and mix with the Romesco sauce. Add the pasta cooking water to make the sauce slightly more liquid and heat everything together. Serve the pasta dish with crispy artichokes on top.

ROMESCO SAUCE

Serves 8   Time 45 min   Difficulty Easy

Ingredients

12–16 ripe tomatoes

2 heads of garlic

1 cup (100 g) toasted almonds

1 cup (100 g) toasted hazelnuts

extra-virgin olive oil

2 tablespoons vinegar

2 tablespoons ñora pepper meat, or the meat from 4 boiled and peeled ñora peppers

½ teaspoon salt

Wash and make a cut in the tomatoes. Bake them with the whole garlic heads for 25 minutes at 390°F (200°C) with 2 tablespoons of olive oil. Once cooked, let them cool and peel the tomatoes and garlic.

Place the tomatoes, garlic, and the rest of the ingredients in a blender. Process and add more oil or fried bread to thicken.

The Romesco sauce can be stored in the refrigerator for a long time and can be consumed with grilled vegetables, baked vegetables, bread, pasta...anything you like!

If you can't find ñora pepper flesh, substitute it with sweet paprika powder, although the flavor will be different.

SWEET AND SOUR WOK WITH TOFU AND PINEAPPLE

The sweetness and acidity of the pineapple elevate this dish to a higher level. This is another classic and easy-to-prepare recipe.

Ingredients

1 cup (200 g) of pineapple

¼ cup each of red, green, and yellow bell pepper (60 g each)

1 large onion

1 small broccoli

1¼ cups (300 g) of tofu

1 tablespoon of cornstarch

oil

Sauce

1 tablespoon of ginger, grated

2 cloves of garlic, chopped

1½ tablespoons of cornstarch

¾ cup (200 ml) of pineapple juice

⅓ cup (100 ml) of water

1 teaspoon of rice vinegar

2 tablespoons of soy sauce (or tamari for a gluten-free version)

1 tablespoon of sweetener (like agave syrup, for example)

Toppings

green onions

chili, chopped

sesame seeds

Serves	Time	Difficulty	High in Protein
2-3	20 min	Easy	

Mix the sauce ingredients in a bowl and set aside.

In a bowl, combine the diced tofu with the cornstarch and sauté with oil until crispy. You can also bake it or use an air fryer.

Sauté the onion in a wok until translucent. Add the chopped bell peppers and the broccoli cut into florets, and sauté until the vegetables soften.

Add the tofu, pineapple, and sauce, and simmer until the sauce thickens and the mixture appears glazed.

Serve with white rice and garnish with green onions, chilies, and sesame seeds.

If you can't find pineapple, use other seasonal fruits: peach, apricot, mango...

BAKED GNOCCHI WITH LENTIL BOLOGNESE

Hanna loves potatoes, so this dish is perfect for her. I love sauces and the Italian style, so this recipe is the ideal middle ground. We adore this baked gnocchi. It is a complete dish, and the grated cheese is vegan, of course! It's the perfect finishing touch for this recipe.

Ingredients

2 cups (500 g) of potatoes

1 cup (150 g) of wheat flour (or another flour if you want them gluten-free)

1 teaspoon of salt

Pepper to taste

Serves	Time	Difficulty	High in Protein
8-10	2 h	Medium	

Boil the potatoes in salted water. Then, drain them, but do not discard the water because it will be used to cook the gnocchi. Mash the potatoes well in a bowl until they become puree.

Add the flour, salt, and pepper to the potatoes, and mix well until you obtain a smooth dough that doesn't stick.

Divide the dough into four pieces on a floured work surface and roll them into logs. Cut them into ½ to ¾-inch (1 or 2 cm) pieces. You can shape them with a fork to give them classic ridges, but this is optional.

Place the gnocchi in boiling water, and when they float in the water, let them boil for 1 more minute. Remove them from the water and set aside.

LENTIL BOLOGNESE SAUCE AND FINISHING

Ingredients

6 large tomatoes, peeled

1 cup (200 g) of lentils, cooked

1 onion, chopped

3 garlic cloves, chopped

1 tablespoon sun-dried tomato paste

2 tablespoons red wine (optional)

fresh basil

vegan mozzarella, diced

vegan cheese, grated

gnocchi

oil

Sauté the onion and garlic in oil. Add the tomatoes and tomato concentrate and fry until they break down. Add the wine and lentils and simmer until the sauce thickens. Incorporate the gnocchi and basil; mix well.

Place the gnocchi and Bolognese in an oven-safe dish and distribute the diced mozzarella in between.

Sprinkle with grated cheese and bake until the cheese is melted.

Try this gnocchi with the
pistachio pesto on page 75.
You'll want more!

Substitute the pine nuts for other nuts, such as walnuts, pistachios, or cashews. Add more oil if you want it to be more liquid.

BEET PESTO PASTA

Ingredients

2¼ cups (250 g) of pasta

beet pesto

vegan feta cheese

fresh basil

Serves | Time | Difficulty
2 | 15 min | Easy

Boil the pasta according to the manufacturer's instructions and cooking times. When finished, drain the pasta.

Mix with the beet pesto.

Serve with vegan feta cheese and chopped basil.

BEET PESTO

Ingredients

2 cups of basil leaves

¼ cup (20 g) of pine nuts, peeled

½ cup (75 g) of beet, cooked

1 clove of garlic

1 teaspoon of salt

juice of ½ lemon

a pinch of pepper

2 tablespoons of nutritional yeast

¼ cup (50 g) of extra-virgin olive oil

Toast the pine nuts in a pan without any fat for a few minutes. Be careful, as they can burn quickly.

Place all the ingredients in a food processor or blender and process until you achieve a homogeneous texture but not a puree.

Transfer the mixture to a glass jar and top with oil to preserve.

HANNA'S CURRY

"This is my all-time favorite curry. I could eat it for breakfast, lunch, or as a dessert. It provides everything I want from a good meal: the sweetness of fruit, the creaminess of coconut milk, vegetables, protein, and curry flavor! It's an absolutely comforting meal, and I hope you enjoy it!" —H.

Ingredients

1 large onion, chopped

2 cup (200 g) spinach, frozen

1½ cup (250 g) chickpeas, cooked and drained

1⅔ cups (400 g) coconut milk, canned

¾ cup (200 ml) vegetable broth

1 cup (150 g) banana, peeled and sliced

1 cup (150 g) apple, peeled and diced

1 cup (150 g) sweet potato, diced

½ teaspoon garam masala

1 teaspoon curry powder

salt and pepper to taste

oil

Serves	Time	Difficulty	Gluten-Free	High in Protein
2-3	30 min	Easy		

Sauté the onion and spinach in a pan with some oil until the spinach defrosts and the onion is softened. You can cover the pan for a few minutes. Add the spices and sauté a few minutes more.

Add the coconut milk and broth; cook for a few more minutes.

Add the banana, apple, sweet potato, and chickpeas, and cook until the sweet potato is soft. It's now ready to enjoy with your favorite sides.

We love to eat it with grated cauliflower, rice, or couscous.

If you have a peanut allergy, prepare the recipe without peanut butter.

THAI BASIL CURRY

Looking for an easy and warm dish? Here's our quick and easy curry made with readily available ingredients!

Ingredients

3 cloves of garlic, chopped

1 tablespoon of ginger, grated

2 tablespoons oil

1½ cups (200 g) tofu or vegan chicken substitute

1⅔ cups (400 ml) coconut milk, canned

2 tablespoons red curry paste

2 tablespoons peanut butter

1 tablespoon soy sauce (or tamari for a gluten-free version)

zest of **1** lime

a handful of Thai basil

Serves	Time	Difficulty	High in Protein	Spicy
2	15 min	Easy		

Sauté the garlic and ginger over medium heat with oil.

Add the red curry paste and sauté for 1 minute.

Add the coconut milk and peanut butter and mix.

Add the previously sautéed tofu or vegan chicken in oil and lime zest and cook on low heat for a few minutes.

Pour in the soy sauce. You can adjust the preparation with more or less sauce. When you get the desired texture, remove from heat and add the basil.

Serve with rice, more basil, and chilies.

If you can't find Thai basil, which has a special flavor, use regular basil leaves. It will have a slightly different taste, but it will be equally delicious.

EASY CURRY PASTE

This recipe is so simple to prepare that it only requires mixing all the ingredients and grinding them in a mortar until you have a smooth, consistent paste. You will need **2** grated garlic cloves, **1 teaspoon** of powdered mustard, **½ teaspoon** powdered cilantro, **1 teaspoon** of powdered turmeric, **1 tablespoon** of grated ginger, zest of **1** lime, juice of **1** lime, **1 tablespoon** of concentrated tomato paste, **1 tablespoon** of powdered cayenne pepper, **½** red bell pepper, **2 tablespoons** of mild olive oil, **1 tablespoon** of sweetener or sugar, and **1 teaspoon** of powdered cumin.

This recipe differs from the original one, as many ingredients are difficult to find. Still, it has a flavor that will satisfy you.

CHICKPEA CURRY WITH NAAN

"There are only a few moments better than coming back to my mom's house and having her prepare this curry. All you need to do is sit at the table and eat. This curry is super easy and quick to prepare, it's high in protein, and it's sweet, salty, and spicy all at the same time." —M.

Ingredients

1 large onion, finely chopped

2 cloves of garlic, chopped

2 carrots, sliced

3 green beans, cut into small pieces

1 small red pepper (2.8 ounces or 80 g), cut into small pieces

2½ **cup**s (400 g) of chickpeas, cooked and drained

1 coconut milk, canned

1¾ **cups** (400 g) of tomatoes, crushed

2 **cups** (500 ml) of vegetable broth

½ **teaspoon** of cinnamon

½ **teaspoon** of sweet paprika

½ **teaspoon** of cumin

1 **teaspoon** of turmeric

1 **tablespoon** of powdered curry

1 **tablespoon** of freshly grated ginger

salt and pepper to taste

oil

Serves 2

Time 20 min

Difficulty Easy

High in Protein

Sauté the onion in a pan with oil until translucent. Add the garlic and all the spices, and fry until fragrant.

Next, add the rest of the vegetables and continue cooking for a few minutes.

Pour in the coconut milk, tomato sauce, and vegetable broth.

Let it simmer for 10 minutes until the sauce thickens and the vegetables are ready. We like them to be crunchy.

Add the cooked chickpeas and mix all the ingredients well.

Serve this curry with white rice, vegan yogurt, and warm naan bread.

 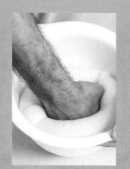 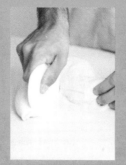 

GARLIC NAAN

Naan

3½ cups (450 g) of strong flour

¾ cup (200 ml) of water

½ cup (100 g) of soy yogurt

1 teaspoon (5 g) of fresh yeast or **½ teaspoon** (2 g) of dry yeast

2 tablespoons (25 g) sweetener or sugar (we use maple syrup)

2 teaspoons (10 g) of salt

Infused Oil

3¼ tablespoons (50 ml) of olive oil

2 garlic cloves, chopped

1 bay leaf

Serves	Prep	Rest	Cooking	Difficulty
8	10 min	2 h 15 min	20 min	Medium

Mix the water, yeast, sweetener, and yogurt. Add the flour and salt and knead for about 10 minutes.

Let the dough rest, covered, for 2 to 3 hours or until it doubles in volume.

Meanwhile, prepare the infused oil by mixing it with the garlic and bay leaf.

Once the dough has risen, divide it into eight parts and form balls. Let them rest, covered, for 15 minutes.

Roll out each ball with a rolling pin until they are about 1/16 inch (2 mm) thick.

For each naan bread, brush one side of the dough with the infused oil and cook in a hot pan for about 2 minutes.

Before flipping the bread, brush the other side, and when bubbles appear, flip and fry for another 2 to 3 minutes.

Wrap the bread in a cloth to keep it warm and enjoy immediately.

GARLIC NAAN

CHICKPEA
CURRY

PALAK TOFU

Originally made with fresh cheese, this traditional Indian dish is prepared with spinach (*palak* means "spinach"). We made our version with tofu and vegan cream cheese. We like to eat it with freshly made naan bread, but you can also serve it with some rice.

Ingredients

1¾ cups (400 g) of spinach

2 cups (300 g) of tofu, baked

1 onion, chopped

2 garlic cloves, chopped

½ **cup** (150 g) of
   tomato puree

½ **cup** (100 g) of vegan
   cream cheese (page 44)

1 teaspoon of ginger, grated

1 tablespoon of brown sugar

1 bay leaf

1 teaspoon of garam masala

salt and pepper

chili powder (optional)

vegan yogurt (topping)

oil

Serves	Time	Difficulty	Gluten-Free	High in Protein
2-3	30 min	Easy		

Sauté the onion in oil until translucent. Add the garlic, ginger, sugar, and spices, and cook for 1 more minute.

Add the spinach and tomato puree; cook until the water is released and the spinach is cooked. Add the cream cheese and stir.

You can process the spinach mixture well with a blender, or lightly, as we like it, for texture.

Serve with the baked tofu, as explained in the above preparation, and a little yogurt. Accompany with freshly made naan bread or rice.

BAKED TOFU

Ingredients

2 cups (300 g) of tofu, cut
   into large pieces

2 **tablespoons** (30 ml)
   of olive oil

½ **teaspoon** of garam masala

¼ **teaspoon** of salt

Mix all the ingredients and marinate the tofu in this preparation.

Bake for 20 minutes at 390°F (200°C). Ready to add to the spinach!

KATSU CURRY

As you may have already noticed, we are lovers of curry and breaded tofu. What can you expect from a dish that combines these two preparations? Nothing less than a fantastic combination.

Tofu Katsu

Serves	Time	Difficulty	High in Protein
4	30 min	Easy	

1½ cups (200 g) of firm tofu

1 cup of breadcrumbs

1 cup of panko (or more breadcrumbs)

½ cup (50 g) of wheat flour

2 teaspoons (10 g) of cornstarch (maicena)

1 teaspoon (5 g) of salt

½ cup (100 ml) of water

½ teaspoon of baking powder

To prepare the crispy tofu, mix the flour, cornstarch, salt, baking powder, and water in a large bowl. These are the necessary ingredients to obtain a vegan egg-like batter.

Cut the tofu into thick slices about ¼ inches (0.5 cm).

Prepare a plate with breadcrumbs and another with panko. Dip each piece of tofu first in the batter, then in the breadcrumbs, back into the batter, and finally in the panko. Place the tofu pieces on a baking tray lined with parchment paper. Bake at 450°F (230°C) for 20 minutes, flipping them every 5 minutes.

CARROT CURRY SAUCE AND FINISH

Ingredients

2 large carrots, grated (about **1 cup**, **7 ounces**, or 200 g)

1 onion, chopped

2 garlic cloves, chopped

olive oil

1 cup (200 ml) of coconut milk

1 cup (200 ml) of vegetable broth

¼ cup (30 g) of raw cashews

1 tablespoon of curry powder

1 teaspoon of salt

Sauté the onion, garlic, and carrots in oil until the carrots begin to soften. Add the curry powder and fry for 1 more minute. Add the cashews, coconut milk, and broth, and simmer for 10 minutes, until the carrots are soft. Adjust the salt to taste.

When the cooking is finished, process everything in a blender or with an immersion blender. If the sauce is too thin, continue cooking for a few more minutes until it reduces.

Serve the crispy tofu katsu with the sauce. Accompany it with white rice and cucumber.

When we prepare this sauce, we always make extra and freeze it, so it's ready to use with anything: rice, vegetables, whatever you like!

FERMÍN'S EXPRESS STEW

"Since I was a child, my father has always cooked spoon food; it's his favorite. And now it's Hanna who always asks him to bring a full container for everyone when he comes to our house." —M.

Ingredients

2½ cups (400 g) of beans, cooked

1 large onion

1 green pepper

½ red pepper

2 carrots

1½ cups (200 g) of smoked tofu

1 tablespoon (15 g) of Pimentón de la Vera (Spanish paprika)

2 cups (500 ml) of vegetable broth

1 bay leaf

1 tablespoon of tomato paste

3 garlic cloves

2 tablespoons of olive oil

salt and pepper to taste

oil

Serves	Time	Difficulty	Gluten-Free	High in Protein
4	30 min	Easy		

Cut the onion, bell peppers, and carrots into medium-sized pieces.

Slice the garlic and dice the tofu.

Pour the oil into a pot and sauté all the vegetables (garlic, onion, bell peppers, and carrots) over medium heat.

After a few minutes, when the vegetables begin to soften, add the paprika, tomato paste, bay leaf, and tofu, and sauté for a few more minutes.

Add the vegetable broth and cook until the vegetables are ready.

Then, add the beans and cook everything together for another 5 minutes. This is the time to adjust the salt and pepper to taste.

After this time, the dish is ready! Enjoy!

This same dish can be prepared with other legumes, such as lentils or chickpeas, and you can add vegetables like spinach or cabbage.

For protein, you can use seitan or soy protein. A 100 percent customizable dish.

TOM KHA SOUP

One of our sources of inspiration for cooking has been traveling to Asia. There, we learned many culinary techniques and a few recipes. That's why we love sharing this Thai soup that captivated us. It has all the flavors, as they claim. It is sweet, salty, spicy, and sour. A delight for any palate.

Ingredients

1¾ cups (400 g) of coconut milk

1¾ cups (400 ml) of vegetable broth or water

1½ cup (200 g) of tofu, cut into large pieces

5 mushrooms, sliced

1 tomato, cut into pieces

1 onion, julienned

1 stalk of lemongrass (or a pinch of lemongrass powder)

¾ inch of fresh ginger, sliced (2 cm)

2 tablespoons (30 ml) of soy sauce

2 teaspoons of sweetener

1 teaspoon of miso paste

1 teaspoon of chili paste

Toppings

fresh cilantro

lime juice

green onion

Serves	Time	Difficulty	Gluten-Free	High in Protein	Spicy
2-3	20 min	Easy			

Bring the coconut milk and water or broth to a boil in a pot. Add the lemongrass, ginger, and chili paste, and boil for 3 more minutes. Add the tofu and boil for another 3 minutes.

Add the onion, tomato, and mushrooms, and let it boil for 5 more minutes.

Turn off the heat and add the remaining ingredients: soy sauce, sweetener, and miso.

Serve in a bowl and complete the soup with cilantro, lime juice, and green onion.

If you can't find lemongrass, substitute it with lime zest. We do this, and it turns out delicious.

OF COU
HUMMU

OUR CREAMIEST HUMMUS

Once you try this hummus, you'll never buy it store-bought again. Never! It's so creamy and unique that you'll always want it ready in the fridge.

Ingredients

1½ cups (200 g) of chickpeas, cooked

1½ cups (200 g) of white beans, cooked

¼ cup (50 ml) of aquafaba or very cold water

½ cup (100 g) of Lebanese tahini

2 tablespoons of lemon juice

¼ teaspoon of cumin

½ teaspoon of salt

½ teaspoon of paprika (optional)

1 clove of garlic (optional)

Toppings

extra-virgin olive oil

flaky salt

sweet or spicy paprika

sesame seeds

Special Occasion Toppings

olives

pickles

cherry tomatoes

parsley

Serves	Time	Difficulty	High in Protein	Gluten-Free
8-10	2 h	Medium		

Process all the ingredients, except the toppings, in a powerful blender until you get a smooth and creamy mixture.

When serving, add the desired toppings for each occasion. You can serve it with Turkish bread (page 81).

Aquafaba is the cooking water of legumes. It's like a thick water.

In this case, we don't use oil, one of the ingredients traditionally used to prepare hummus. Instead, we use Lebanese tahini, which has a mild flavor and is quite liquid. If you can't find Lebanese tahini, add oil and reduce the amount of tahini.

A tip for making the hummus creamier is to use all cold ingredients from the fridge. Another way is to use ice cubes instead of water.

PIQUILLO PEPPER
HUMMUS

ROASTED CARROT
HUMMUS

OUR CRACKERS

ROASTED CARROT HUMMUS

When carrots are roasted, they become very sweet and give the hummus a pleasant, sweet touch that we love.

Ingredients

2 cups (250 g) of cooked chickpeas, drained

¼ cup (50 ml) of aquafaba or water

2¼ cups (300 g) of roasted carrots

2 tablespoons (30 g) of tahini

2 cloves of roasted garlic

juice of ½ lemon

½ teaspoon of curry powder

½ teaspoon of salt

a drizzle of extra-virgin olive oil

Serves	Time	Difficulty	High in Protein	Gluten-Free
4	40 min	Easy		

Roast the carrots and garlic in the oven at 400°F (200°C) for 30 minutes.

Put all the ingredients in a blender.

Process until you get a smooth cream. You can add more oil if desired.

You can achieve a similar hummus with roasted pumpkin if you want to prepare a special winter recipe.

PIQUILLO PEPPER HUMMUS

This is our hummus for special occasions. We love the slightly sweet and smoky touch that piquillo peppers provide. (PS: Piquillo is a cooked red pepper!) Don't hold back and give it a try.

Ingredients

2 cups (250 g) of cooked and drained chickpeas

3¼ tablespoons (50 ml) of aquafaba or water

6 piquillo peppers

3 tablespoons of extra-virgin olive oil

2 cloves of garlic

juice of ½ lemon

½ teaspoon of paprika

½ teaspoon of salt

Serves	Time	Difficulty	High in Protein	Gluten-Free
4	5 min	Easy		

Sauté the piquillo peppers and 2 garlic cloves in a pan with oil.

Add them to the blender along with the rest of the ingredients.

Process until you get a smooth cream. Add more oil or aquafaba if you want a smoother texture.

OUR CRACKERS

These crackers are the result of a mistake in a flatbread recipe we wanted to make. We forgot the bread in the oven and it toasted toot much. As a result, we got some incredible crackers. They accompany all the hummus we make.

Ingredients

¾ cup (100 g) of spelt flour

2 cups (250 g) of whole wheat flour

1¼ teaspoon (8 g) of fresh yeast

1 cup (250 ml) of soy drink, cold

2 teaspoons (10 g) of olive oil

2 teaspoons (9 g) of brown sugar

1¼ teaspoons (7 g) of salt

Serves	Prep	Rest	Cooking	Difficulty
6	10 min	1 hr	20 min	Easy

Mix all the ingredients in a bowl without kneading. Cover and let rest for at least 1 hour.

Preheat the oven to 400°F (200°C).

Form balls and roll out the dough (it's easier than rolling out all the dough at once). Place them on the tray, cut them into the desired shape, and make holes with a fork.

Bake for 15 to 20 minutes at 400°F (200°C). Let them cool and break them! They are the best companions for hummus.

AVOCADO AND PEA HUMMUS

This is more than just a green hummus; we call it our protein-packed guacamole or green spirit hummus. It has a flavor similar to guacamole, perhaps identical, but you get an extra serving of protein thanks to the chickpeas and peas. We love it!

Serves	Time	Difficulty	High in Protein	Gluten-Free
4	5 min	Easy		

Ingredients

2 cups (250 g) of chickpeas, cooked and drained

½ cup (100 g) of avocado

1 cup (150 g) of peas

¼ cup (50 g) of tahini

1 tablespoon (15 g) of olive oil

¼ cup (50 g) of aquafaba or water

juice of ½ lemon

½ fresh garlic clove

a handful of fresh cilantro

1 teaspoon of salt

a pinch of pepper

Toppings

tomatoes

cilantro

olive oil

If using frozen peas, thaw and cook them for a few minutes. Once cooked, drain and let them cool.

Peel the avocado and cut it into pieces.

Process the peas, avocado, chickpeas, and the rest of the ingredients in a powerful blender until you get a smooth cream.

Add the suggested toppings or others of your liking and enjoy!

Serves	Time	Difficulty	High in Protein	Gluten-Free
4	5 min	Easy		

Ingredients

2½ cups (400 g) of lentils, cooked and drained

¼ cup (50 g) of tahini

¼ cup (50 g) of aquafaba or water

1 tablespoon (15 g) of olive oil

juice of ½ lemon

½ teaspoon of cumin

1 teaspoon of salt

a pinch of pepper

Process all the ingredients in a blender until you get a smooth cream.

BEET HUMMUS

This is one of our favorite hummus recipes. It makes any meal feel special.

Ingredients

2 cups (250 g) of chickpeas

½ cup (100 g) of beet, cooked

¼ cup (50 g) of tahini

¼ cup (50 g) of aquafaba or water

½ ounce (15 g) of olive oil

½ fresh garlic clove

juice of ½ lemon

½ teaspoon of cumin

1 teaspoon of salt

Serves	Time	Difficulty	High in Protein	Gluten-Free
4	5 min	Easy		

Process all the ingredients in a powerful blender until you get a smooth cream.

MANGO AND CURRY HUMMUS

This unique hummus variation adds a touch of sweetness and spice to the traditional recipe, making it a perfect choice for those looking for something different.

Ingredients

2 cups (250 g) of chickpeas

¼ cup (50 g) of tahini

¼ cup (50 g) of plant-based yogurt

¼ cup (50 g) of aquafaba or water

½ mango

juice of ½ lemon

1 teaspoon of curry powder

½ teaspoon of turmeric

1 teaspoon of salt

Serves	Time	Difficulty	High in Protein	Gluten-Free
4	5 min	Easy		

Peel and dice the ripe mango.

Process the mango, chickpeas, and the rest of the ingredients in a powerful blender until you get a smooth cream.

Serve with your choice of toppings or enjoy as is!

LENTIL HUMMUS

MANGO AND CURRY HUMMUS

BEET HUMMUS

AVOCADO AND PEA HUMMUS

SWEETEN YOUR DAY

CHOCOLATE BABKA

This sweet bread called babka (which means "grandmother" in several Slavic languages) is known for its beautiful, braided shape. It's easy to make, fluffy, and can be filled in many ways. You'll leave everyone speechless!

Ingredients

4 cups (500 g) of wheat flour

1¼ cups (300 ml) of plant-based milk

3 tablespoons (40 g) of sugar

1½ tablespoons (20 g) of fresh yeast

½ teaspoon of salt

¼ cup (60 g) of mild olive oil or other neutral-flavored oil

½ cup (100 g) of vegan chocolate cream

Serves	Time	Rest	Difficulty	High in Protein	Gluten-Free
10	1 hr	1 hr 30 min	Medium		

Dissolve the yeast with plant-based milk and sugar in a bowl. If you prefer, you can use dry yeast but in a smaller quantity.

Add the rest of the ingredients, except the chocolate spread, and mix.

Knead until you get a soft and non-sticky dough.

Form a ball and place it in the bowl, cover with a damp cloth (or plastic bag) and let it rest for about 1 hour, until it doubles in size.

Prepare a rectangular cake or bread pan.

Roll out the dough into a rectangular shape, about ¼-inch thick. Spread the chocolate cream and roll it lengthwise.

With a sharp knife, cut the roll in half lengthwise.

Join the ends and start "braiding" the dough, one over the other, always keeping the cut side facing up.

Press lightly and place the braid in the pan.

Let it rest for another 30 minutes, covered with a cloth, and in the meantime, preheat the oven to 350°F.

Brush the braid with a little more plant-based milk and sugar and bake for 35 minutes.

Instead of chocolate spread as a filling, you can also use any nut butter or jam.

CRUNCHY BARS WITH TWO CHOCOLATES

We've always loved those Crunch candy bars that are popular in American movie theaters, but they contain ingredients that aren't healthy—lots of sugar and preservatives—and they're not vegan. That's why we created our slightly more nutritious but incredibly delicious version. Have you ever seen a two-colored chocolate? Amazing!

Ingredients

½ **cup** (100 g) of white chocolate, vegan

1 teaspoon of coconut oil

1¼ **cup**s (200 g) of dark chocolate, 70 percent, vegan

1½ **ounces** (40 g) of puffed rice, unsweetened

¼ **cup** (50 g) of hazelnut cream or other nut cream

a pinch of salt

Serves	Time	Difficulty	Gluten-Free
8	20 min	Easy	

Melt the white chocolate in a saucepan and mix it with the coconut oil.

Fill a square mold or bar mold with the previous mixture to create the top layer of the nougat. Let it cool in the refrigerator while you melt the dark chocolate.

Combine the melted dark chocolate with the salt and hazelnut cream; remove from heat. Mix with the puffed rice. Fill the rest of the mold with the white chocolate. Let it cool at room temperature or in the refrigerator.

When it solidifies, remove it from the mold and store it in an airtight container at room temperature. Enjoy!

You can also use chocolate puffed rice, but keep in mind that you may need to adjust the quantity.

If you want to cook gluten-free, make sure the ingredients you bought do not contain gluten.

THREE PROTEIN MOUSSES

This is the best dessert if you want to prepare something easy, that everyone likes, that can be eaten on both a cold winter day or a hot summer day, and above all, healthy and rich in protein. We love this dessert in every way, and these are our three favorite flavors.

CHOCOLATE MOUSSE

Serves	Time	Rest	Difficulty	High in Protein
2	5 min	20 min	Easy	

Ingredients

1½ cups (200 g) of silken tofu

¼ cup (50 g) of 75 percent cocoa dark chocolate (vegan)

1 tablespoon of maple syrup

additional chopped vegan chocolate for topping

Melt the chocolate using a double boiler. In the meantime, process the tofu and sweetener with a blender. Then, add the melted chocolate and blend again until well mixed.

Pour the mixture into 2 cups or glasses and let it cool in the refrigerator for at least 2 hours before consuming.

Serve this mousse with chopped chocolate on top.

BLUEBERRY MOUSSE

Ingredients

1½ cups (200 g) of silken tofu

¾ cup (100 g) of blueberries

1 tablespoon of maple syrup

additional blueberries for topping

Process all the ingredients in a blender.

Pour the mixture into 2 cups or glasses and let it cool in the refrigerator for at least 2 hours before consuming.

Serve with more blueberries on top.

CHEESECAKE MOUSSE

Ingredients

1½ cups (200 g) of silken tofu

¼ cup (50 g) of vegan cream cheese

1 tablespoon of maple syrup

¼ teaspoon of vanilla extract

2–3 cookies

jam for topping

Blend the tofu, vegan cheese, maple syrup, and vanilla in a blender.

Crumble two cookies into a glass or cup and pour in the mousse.

Chill in the refrigerator for a minimum of 2 hours before serving.

Serve with another cookie and your choice of jam.

This mousse can be prepared
with any berry or fruit you
desire or that is in season.

SALTY CHOCOLATE COOKIES

We've always loved the combination of sweet and salty, mainly chocolate and salt. That's how these cookies came to life. We often make salty cookies to enjoy with our hummus and eat them with chocolate spread. These cookies, which contain salt, tahini, and chocolate, are an addictive and healthy treat.

Ingredients

1½ **cup**s (200 g) of spelt flour

1 **cup** (100 g) of almond flour

1½ **tablespoons** of baking powder

1 **teaspoon** of salt

2 **tablespoons** of olive oil

½ **cup** (100 ml) of water

2 **tablespoons** of Lebanese tahini (liquid)

Toppings

¼ **cup** (50 g) of melting chocolate (vegan)

flaked salt

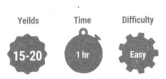

Yeilds 15-20

Time 1 hr

Difficulty Easy

Preheat the oven to 390°F (200°C).

Mix all the dry ingredients in a large bowl.

Add the oil, water, and tahini, and knead with your hands until everything is well incorporated. The dough should be dry but moldable. If it is too dry, add more oil to the mixture.

Form balls with your hands or roll out the dough and cut the cookies with a cookie cutter.

Place them on a baking tray lined with parchment paper and bake for 20 minutes, until they start to brown.

In the meantime, melt the chocolate.

Once the cookies are baked, dip the bottom of each cookie in the chocolate and place them back on the tray until the chocolate solidifies.

Drizzle any remaining chocolate over the cookies and sprinkle with flaked salt.

MANGO STICKY RICE VEGAN CHEESECAKE

One of our favorite desserts is mango sticky rice from Thailand. It's a delightful combination of sticky rice with coconut, fresh mango, and a sweet and salty coconut sauce. This cheesecake is inspired by that recipe and brings back memories of afternoons spent in Thailand.

Base

1¼ cups (150 g) of vegan white chocolate

½ cup (50 g) of puffed rice

For the Filling

2 cups (250 g) of vegan cream cheese (page 44)

1 can of coconut milk (13½ ounces or 400 ml)

3 tablespoons of sweetener

1 teaspoon (3 g) of agar-agar

½ teaspoon of salt

For the Topping

½ ripe mango

½ teaspoon (1 g) of agar-agar

½ cup (100 ml) of water

2 tablespoons of sweetener

Serves	Time	Difficulty	Gluten-Free
8	1 hr	Medium	

Melt the white chocolate using a double boiler and prepare an 18 cm (about 7 inches) round cake pan lined with parchment paper.

Mix the white chocolate with the puffed rice and press it into the base of the mold. Chill in the refrigerator so the white chocolate solidifies.

Separate the fat from the coconut water. To do this, put the can in the refrigerator a few hours in advance so that the fat hardens and is easy to separate. Set aside separately.

Thoroughly mix the coconut fat with the cream cheese, salt, and sweetener in a bowl until there are no lumps.

Mix 1 teaspoon of agar-agar with the coconut water in a saucepan and boil for 2 minutes at high heat to activate the agar-agar. After 2 minutes, pour the contents of the saucepan into the bowl with the other ingredients. Stir with a whisk until everything is integrated. Quickly pour the contents into the mold to form the filling layer. Allow it to cool for 1 hour in the refrigerator before preparing the topping.

For the topping, blend the mango with the sweetener in a hand blender and puree.

Mix ½ teaspoon of agar-agar and approximately ½ cup of water in a saucepan and boil for 2 minutes to activate the agar-agar. Then, combine it with the mango puree and immediately pour it into the mold. Allow it to cool for 1 hour, and the cake will be ready.

PEANUT AND CHOCOLATE COOKIES

These are some of our favorite cookies. We love this combination of peanut and chocolate. And who doesn't? They have an extra dose of protein, making them a perfect snack for any time of day.

Ingredients

1½ cups (150 g) of oat flour

¼ cup (30 g) of vanilla-flavored protein powder

¼ cup (60 g) of coconut sugar

½ teaspoon of baking powder

½ tablespoon of salt

¼ teaspoon of vanilla extract

¾ cup (180 g) of peanut butter

½ cup (120 ml) of plant-based milk

¼ cup (30 g) of chopped toasted peanuts

¼ cup (30 g) of vegan dark chocolate chips

Serves	Time	Difficulty	High in Protein
6-8	30 min	Easy	

Preheat the oven to 350°F (175°C).

Mix the flour, protein, sugar, baking powder, and salt in a bowl.

Add the rest of the ingredients and mix well. Add more plant-based milk if necessary.

To prepare the cookies, form balls with your hands, place them on a baking tray lined with parchment paper and press them down slightly.

Bake for about 20 minutes or until golden.

You can use more oat flour to avoid using protein powder.

CHICKPEA BLONDIES

We love these little protein-rich snacks. They are sweet and very delicious. We eat them for breakfast, but they also serve as a great snack between meals. You won't even realize you're eating legumes!

Ingredients

2 cups (250 g) of cooked and drained chickpeas

2 tablespoons of peanut butter

1 tablespoon of sweetener

2 tablespoons of plant-based milk

1 teaspoon of baking powder

a pinch of salt

¼ cup (30 g) of vegan chocolate chips

Serves	Time	Difficulty	High in Protein
6	40 min	Easy	

Preheat the oven to 350°F (180°C).

Place all the ingredients except the chocolate and salt in a food processor and blend until you have a thick and consistent mixture.

Add the chocolate (saving a few chips) and the salt; incorporate well.

Pour into a small square or rectangular baking dish and press down until the mixture is about ½ to 1-inch (1 to 2 cm) thick.

Add the remaining chocolate and salt. Bake for 30 minutes.

After baking, allow it to cool so it firms up and doesn't fall apart.

Substitute chickpeas with other legumes, such as beans.

Prepare crispy chickpeas as a savory snack, using the spices of your choice and without chocolate.

CHOCOLATE-COVERED CRISPY CHICKPEAS

Chickpeas are an absolute all-rounder for us; they're our primary ingredient. They're packed with proteins and significant amounts of calcium and magnesium. With them, you can make everything from the creamiest hummus to the crunchiest snacks. And yes, you can also make sweets with them. We love them, and they are outstanding with chocolate.

Ingredients

¾ **cup** (110 g) of crispy chickpeas

½ **cup** (110 g) of 70 percent cacao dark chocolate (vegan)

salt flakes

Serves	Time	Difficulty	High in Protein	Gluten-Free
20	1 hr	Easy		

Melt the chocolate in a double boiler and add the crispy chickpeas you've prepared beforehand.

Stir well with a spoon to ensure they are all well coated with chocolate.

Then, prepare a baking tray lined with parchment paper or any flat surface, and spoon out a portion of chickpeas. Move it to the tray for the chickpeas to cool. Proceed this way until all chickpeas are used.

Add some salt flakes for the perfect final touch.

CRISPY CHICKPEAS

Ingredients

1 **cup** of dry chickpeas

½ **teaspoon** of salt

1 **tablespoon** of oil

Soak the chickpeas for at least 8 hours.

Then, drain them and pat them dry with a towel. Mix the chickpeas well in a bowl with the salt and oil.

Transfer them to a baking tray and bake for 30 minutes at 450°F (230°C), stirring every 10 minutes. The baking time can be up to 45 minutes, depending on the size of the chickpeas.

Let them cool to become extra crispy.

BANANA BREAD WITH TAHINI

Our all-time favorite treat! The best thing to always have in your kitchen: a delicious banana bread! It's a beautiful breakfast with nut butter or jam; it serves as a great snack between meals. We take it on trips and give it to our child for breakfast at daycare.

Ingredients

1½ **cups** (180 g) of wheat flour

2 teaspoons of baking powder

½ **teaspoon** of baking soda

⅓ **cup** (70 g) of brown sugar

¾ **cup** (180 g) of bananas, very ripe and mashed

3 tablespoons (40 ml) of plant-based milk

⅓ **cup** (70 g) of liquid tahini

1½ **tablespoons** (20 g) of neutral-flavor oil

a splash of lemon juice or vinegar

1 chia egg (**1 tablespoon** of ground chia + **3 tablespoons** of water)

1 teaspoon of cinnamon (optional)

¼ **cup** (30 g) of walnuts (optional)

¼ **cup** (30 g) of raisins (optional)

1 banana for topping (optional)

If you don't have tahini at home, replace it with ¼ cup of neutral-flavor oil.

Serves	Time	Difficulty
8	1 hr	Easy

Preheat the oven to 350°F (180°C) and line a rectangular loaf pan (10 x 5 inches, 25 x 12 cm) with parchment paper.

Prepare the chia egg in a small bowl by mixing the chia with water and set aside.

Sift the flour and mix all the dry ingredients in a large bowl.

Add the wet ingredients and the chia egg; incorporate well to ensure there are no lumps.

Add optional ingredients, except for the banana reserved for the topping: nuts, seeds, dried fruit, or spices, and mix well.

Fill the loaf pan with the batter and decorate with banana slices, more crushed walnuts, or your favorite toppings, and bake for 50 minutes.

Remove from the oven and let it cool for at least 1 hour before cutting.

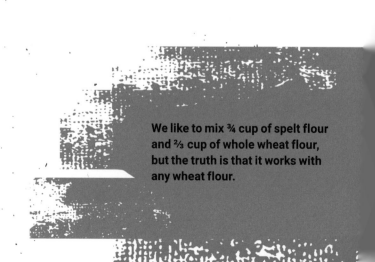

We like to mix ¾ cup of spelt flour and ⅔ cup of whole wheat flour, but the truth is that it works with any wheat flour.

ACKNOWLEDGMENTS

"What a journey!" as Hanna would say.

Creating this book has been a beautiful, inspiring, stressful, and utterly unique experience for us, and it wouldn't have been possible without the help of some special people to whom we'd like to express our gratitude.

First and foremost, we want to thank you, who holds this book in your hands, for taking this step and wanting to delve into our world and our kitchen. This book will help you improve and enjoy a 100 percent plant-based cuisine.

We want to thank everyone in our community who has supported us from the minute they knew about the AddictedToHummus project.

We want to express our gratitude to Mercè (Manel's mother) and her partner Jordi, who have made a one-hour car journey to our house every Saturday for weeks and weeks to help us manage a kitchen, a baby, and a dog. While we started the day early preparing the kitchen, the ingredients, and the recipes, Mercè and Jordi entertained Nalu and Mali for hours so we could experiment, cook, take photos, and try new recipes. Granted, they didn't leave empty-handed. After each day, we sat at the table to eat what we had prepared.

To Fermín (Manel's father), who has been co-creating recipes with us, offering his tricks, tasting, and giving his valuable opinion. He is a chef and, undoubtedly, one of our most demanding customers. He is our biggest fan, and we are profoundly grateful and honored for his endless support.

To our neighbors, who have also been helping us. They've tasted what we've cooked for the book and have given us their preferences, opinions, and desires. It has been a pleasure sharing meals with you!

We sincerely thank Gloria for writing the foreword and making the book even more special. Also, to Miquel and our families, you are an essential part of our journey and a reference for us and the entire community.

Last but not least, we want to thank Maria Àngels, Esther, Enrique, and the rest of the Larousse team for making this project a reality, which we have shaped together. Without them, none of this would have been possible. We know we are not the easiest authors, always pursuing every detail. Still, we are confident that we have achieved a unique book, one we love and that truly reflects our style and character.

ABOUT THE AUTHORS

Hanna Buschmann worked as a materials developer for various sports brands, but soon felt that she needed to turn her life around. She left that industry and joined her partner Manel García to create the *Addicted to Hummus* blog to share their experiences on vegan food and recipes. A great lover of fitness, yoga, and a conscious lifestyle, Hanna is also a great traveler and has lived in different places. Street food and local dishes from the places she has visited have inspired her in her quest to fuel her body mindfully and vegan. Manel and Hanna met in Barcelona and traveled throughout Europe and Asia; they are still traveling.

Manel García Prats has a degree in industrial engineering but has never practiced as such. He has been passionate about cooking since he was a child due to the influence of his father Fermín and in his early days he worked in the world of hospitality. In 2017, together with his partner Hanna Buschmann, they decided to take the step to veganism and in 2020 they began to share all those recipes that they were learning and developing on social networks with great success. Shortly after, *Addicted to Hummus* was born, a project, blog, and now a book where they share easy, colorful, rich, and vegan recipes daily.

Mango Publishing, established in 2014, publishes an eclectic list of books by diverse authors—both new and established voices—on topics ranging from business, personal growth, women's empowerment, LGBTQ studies, health, and spirituality to history, popular culture, time management, decluttering, lifestyle, mental wellness, aging, and sustainable living. We were named 2019 and 2020's #1 fastest growing independent publisher by Publishers Weekly. Our success is driven by our main goal, which is to publish high-quality books that will entertain readers as well as make a positive difference in their lives.

Our readers are our most important resource; we value your input, suggestions, and ideas. We'd love to hear from you—after all, we are publishing books for you!

Please stay in touch with us and follow us at:

Facebook: Mango Publishing
Twitter: @MangoPublishing
Instagram: @MangoPublishing
LinkedIn: Mango Publishing
Pinterest: Mango Publishing
Newsletter: mangopublishinggroup.com/newsletter

Join us on Mango's journey to reinvent publishing, one book at a time.